WORKING AT HOME

Lindsey O'Connor

D1280208

HARVEST HOUSE PUBLISHERS

EUGENE, OREGON

Scripture quotations are taken from the New American Standard Bible®, © 1960, 1962, 1963, 1968, 1971, 1972, 1973, 1975, 1977 by The Lockman Foundation. Used by permission. (www.Lockman.org)

Cover by Terry Dugan Design, Minneapolis, Minnesota

WORKING AT HOME

Published by Harvest House Publishers
Eugene, Oregon 97402
www.harvesthousepublishers.com

Library of Congress Cataloging-in-Publication Data
  O'Connor, Lindsey, 1961–
    Working at home / Lindsey O'Connor
        p. cm.
  Rev. ed. of: Working at home. ©1990.
  ISBN 0-7369-1371-8
  1. Home-based businesses. I. O'Connor, Lindsey, 1961–   . Working at home. II. Title.
HD2333.033 1997
658'.041—dc21   97-12970
                                                                                      CIP

Printed in the United States of America

       03   04   05   06   07   08   09   10   / BP-CF /   10 9 8 7 6 5 4 3 2

To the five biggest reasons I work at home:
Jacquelyn, Claire, Collin, Allison, and Caroline.
And to Tim, for giving me the inspiration
that day at our kitchen table to start a home business.

Contents

1

Working at Home: Beyond a Trend

Peg writes and edits full-time. Posy sells cross-stitch kits to museum gift shops around the country. Carol's family builds and sells computers. Eileen is an artist who designs greeting cards. Gail is a publicist working for a major recording company. What do all of these people have in common? They are all successful—and they all work from home.

At one time working from home was an intriguing trend, something new on the business scene as an alternative work option. But today you don't have to look very far to find someone who's making working from home work for them. Some people want to skip the commute and office protocol. Others are tired of working for someone else. Countless numbers want the privilege of raising their own children and are searching for a way to avoid full-time child care. Others have simply given up the corporate rat race. Many are nurturing a part-time solution to their financial problems. More than a few are building successful careers and creating tremendously profitable businesses. And some, as one home-worker put it, just want to be able to cut big-dollar deals over the phone while wearing their pajamas and bunny slippers.

Working from home is a dream for many people, and it was my dream as well. But, since the start, I have often found it difficult to juggle my role as wife, mother, and worker—and I know I'm not the only one! Especially at the beginning, I felt so much conflict between the need and desire to be with my children, the cash crunch, my desire to be a helpmate to my husband, and even my ambition. Yet in God's goodness and perfect timing, He has allowed my dream to become a reality. Along with millions of others, I work from home. Perhaps you can, too. This book was born out of a desire to give you the encouragement, motivation, and tools necessary to make it happen. Whether you're the primary breadwinner, or you're looking for a way to pursue your dreams, or you need a supplemental income to enable one parent to be home with the children, working from home can be a wonderful option. Perhaps you can identify with some of the following people.

• Gail loved her job, but becoming pregnant was an answer to her prayers. "My problem then," said Gail, "was the conflict of those two dreams. I told my husband that I didn't want to work and let someone else raise my child from 7:00 A.M. until 6:00 P.M. I didn't want someone else telling me about my baby's first steps or first words. I had to either quit my job or convince my employer that working from home would benefit us both. God intervened, and now I work at home. It's not the easiest path, but it's the best option for all of us—me, my employer, and my baby. And I got to witness Tanner's first steps, not just hear about them!"

• Many people simply love the idea that going to work means walking across the hall. Gary said, "I feel sorry for all those people who have to get up and go somewhere every day. Whenever I have early-morning meetings and am forced to join the other rush-hour commuters, I wonder how people can spend an hour or two on the road every day commuting. To own a business and be locked in traffic is the most frustrating thing in the world—even with a cell phone. Working at home is great. People who call don't know whether I have 20 employees and am wearing a tie or not!"

• For others, running a business from a home-based office allows them to pursue God's leading and keep family a priority. When Liz became pregnant with her first child, she was working six days a week in radio and giving 90 speeches a year. "I knew I couldn't continue to do both jobs well and be a mother," she said. "Something had to go, and it wasn't going to be the child!" So she left a stable, full-time career to go out on her own from a home-based office and has been speaking and writing on her own for many years, making ten times what she made in radio.

• Barbara has always had high goals for her career, but after having children she had to find a balance. She wanted to be, in her words, a "traditional at-home mommy" without giving up her dreams forever. "I know that I need to be home with my children during this early period for their spiritual, emotional, and intellectual growth. I know I could be working full-time outside to further my career, but working mainly out of my home is what I need to do right now. I know the Lord will provide in my business when His time is right."

Working from home—whether full-time or part-time, as an entrepreneur or for someone else—has moved from trend to mainstream. People who have chosen a home-based work option are still making crafts, sewing, and selling, but they're also running prosperous service businesses, telecommuting for large corporations, producing radio programs from home studios, and navigating the online world. They're combining their skills, experiences, and passions to create businesses that target very specific markets. They're using ever-changing technological advances to make their work easier or even possible. They're finding outlets for their creativity and alternatives to retirement. Many are finally pursuing their dreams, assessing their gifts and strengths, and then boldly stepping out as God leads them.

If you are considering joining their ranks, you're not alone. Statistics vary widely, but IDC/LINK, a market research firm that tracks the home-business industry, reports that over 30 million people work from home offices either part-time or full-time, and over 20 million earned income from full-time or part-time self employment. Although government-related statistics are lower, all projections suggest that the number of home-based workers will continue to increase.

Not that long ago, those of us who worked from home had to work a little harder to be taken seriously in some circles. Today, however, prime-time television commercials reflect our society's shift towards mainstreaming this career option. I remember the first time I saw such an ad. My husband Tim said, "Honey, come in here. You'll want to see this." A small-business machine manufacturer was talking about (and targeting) people who work at home. I thought, "Aha, now we're no longer an anomaly! We're a viable industry! I hope my neighbors are watching this." Since then, such ads are anything but rare.

But home-business owners are not the only ones opting to work where they live. Many corporations offer some employees the opportunity to telecommute—to work out of their homes but be linked electronically to the corporate office. Continuing technological advances and the affordability of home-office equipment are allowing the number of telecommuters to increase. Whether a self-employed entrepreneur, a telecommuter, a pieceworker (a person in industrial or textile work paid by the piece), or an independent contractor working for a company without employee rights or benefits, many people choose the home-based work option, and they do so for a variety of reasons.

The Motivation

The overriding reasons why people in the traditional workforce get in their cars every day and drive to work are to earn a paycheck and to advance in their career. Additional factors (we'll look at six) motivate people choosing to work from home, and the underlying theme is control. Working from home simply allows a person greater control. That comes as people working out of their home benefit from having more family time, greater flexibility, no commute, reduced stress, less office protocol, increased productivity, and the opportunity to pursue success as they define it.

1. *More Family Time*

Without a doubt, the number one reason I work from home myself and recommend it wholeheartedly is because it enables me to put my family ahead of my career. Former President George H. Bush once said, "I believe that family and faith represent the moral compass of the nation, and I'll work to make them strong. For as Benjamin Franklin said, 'If the sparrow cannot fall to the ground without His notice, can a great nation rise without His aid?'" We must make every effort to foster strong families and strong faith and personal freedoms that allow flexibility and creativity in our work options. Our country's wave of downshifting (evidence that people are voluntarily choosing simplicity) shows that both men and women are doing just that. Surveys continue to show that more and more people are looking for ways to spend more time with their families, even if that means sacrificing a promotion or prestige at the office. Many are finding that working from home provides the solution.

Traditional families where children are raised by parents instead of child care workers are truly a blessing, yet that ideal is not always possible. Divorce and death, among other things, often force many women into the workforce when they'd rather not be there. One study reported that 87 percent of mothers said they'd prefer to spend more time with their children.[2] For these women, who want to be with their children more but feel they can't, I get especially excited about the home-based option. If you're one of the vast number of women in the workforce and you'd either rather not be there, or you want to cut back, or you simply want to spend more time with your children, I encourage you to seriously consider working from home. This option might be right for you.

This work option might also be in your future if you're a single parent. First let me say that I have a great deal of empathy for you. In the past, my husband traveled a great deal, and his absence Monday through Friday left me feeling like a single parent. As hard as those times were, I know that they truly don't compare to the struggle many single parents face as they try to provide for their family's needs. If you are a single parent, God may open a new door of possibilities for you as you investigate the option of working from home. (And know that, before this book reached your hands, I prayed for you. I asked God to guide and direct you, to open doors and even close doors, because home businesses aren't for everyone.)

Then there are the corporate moms who enjoy being where they are yet feel the tug to be at home. In the past the so-called "mommy track" in the corporate world (as opposed to the fast track) gained fame with reports of understanding bosses, job sharing, flex-time, and time off for childbirth and infant-raising without sacrificing potential and position on the corporate ladder. While those benefits for working mothers were good, home-businesses offer advantages over the mommy track, which perpetuated the idea that fulfilled, successful women are corporate women who just happen to slow down a bit. One article reported, "Many women believe they can slow down at work for a few years, get their kids launched, and come back with renewed zest."[3] But children are not rockets needing to be launched; children are gifts from the Lord needing to be nurtured over time. With the shift away from the mommy track, many women turned their gaze from the corporate ladder with its glass ceiling toward entrepreneurial efforts.

Other parents need additional income or want to pursue their career while remaining the primary caregiver for their children. Working at home gives them more time to enjoy and nurture their little gifts from the Lord. While working at home during the preschool years is indeed a challenge, it is also a privilege: You have the opportunity to be the main molder of character in your child's life, not just in the evenings and on weekends. You also have an opportunity to be available to older children and teenagers after school.

One in-home childcare provider has reaped many benefits from putting her family first: "When I worked outside the home, the housework was never caught up, dinner was always late, and there was never enough family time. Now that I'm home, I can do my job during the day and fit the housework around it. Then, when my husband comes home and the daycare kids leave, we can have a nice, relaxed evening together. The very best reward of all, though, is being with my son and seeing him grow and learn. I'm glad I didn't have to miss that."

So what should we call those of us moms who work at home in order to spend more time with our family? How about "mompreneurs"? In a book by that title, Ellen Parlapiano and Patricia Cobe write, "Being more accessible to your kids means more of a chance to watch them grow; more time to develop positive, nurturing relationships; and more involvement in their lives....Mompreneurs can set their own schedules, establish their own income goals, advance at their own pace, and never be fired for fulfilling family commitments first."[4]

Working at home is a wonderful opportunity for men as well as women. Some men work at home full-time through their own businesses. Some telecommute. And others who do some of their work at home find that the home office allows them to be with their families more when the corporate office expects overtime. Some male-dominated professions lend themselves especially well to partial home-based work. Home-based employment allows men to become more involved in family life, a real plus for those families and for society in general. As one home business advocate said, "Men or women, it may not be possible in every situation to work exclusively at home, but certainly the more home-based work we can provide, the better the opportunities for our families."[5]

2. *Greater Flexibility*

The freedom to decide when and how you'll work—in a word, flexibility—is one of the biggest advantages of working at home. Technically, you get to set your own schedule. As many home-business owners know, however, sometimes it feels as if the business and its deadlines set our schedules for us. Yet we still have an element of control, and that control gives us great freedom and reduces our stress. Self-imposed and even client-driven deadlines give us greater control in our lives than punching a company time clock.

After all, no policy manual dictates when the workday begins or ends or at what time coffee breaks are allowed. You needn't fear using up an allotted number of sick days, and you don't have to be employed for a year before you can take a vacation. If little Johnny is the giant carrot in the school play and the curtain goes up at two in the afternoon, you can be there. Or if you feel like burning the midnight oil or taking some time off so you can help with your church's vacation Bible school, you can decide to do just that. Many self-employed home-basers put in more hours each week than those punching someone else's clock, but they decide *if* they want to and *when* they want to.

Judy, a home-based calligrapher, says, "I love being able to work around school schedules, my Bible study, and volunteer work. I also like the fact that [my work] is part-time."

One home-worker I know gets up at four-thirty each morning and puts in at least three hours at her business before changing hats to take care of her family. After the kids are at school and her husband is at work, she's back at it until three in the afternoon. That way she is able to work full-time, yet be home and available for her family when they need her.

And then there are those (like me) who tend to find their creative juices flowing late at night. If I choose to stay up, I don't have to think about being dressed and alert for the business world at the crack of dawn. Yet sometimes I'll work early before the kids are up. The flexibility to do both is freeing. I love deciding if I'm going to work early or late and still be able to take the kids to gymnastics or gather the brood and go for a walk!

3. *No Commute*

How would you like to have an additional 20 hours a month? Think of all you could do with those extra hours! Since there will never be a 36-hour day, you'll probably never find those additional hours unless you're now a commuter who's about to start working from home. On average, people commute 30 minutes to their place of employment. That's five hours a week or 20 hours a month that, once you're not commuting, you can do with as you wish. It's time for playing with the kids, reading a book, going on a family outing, enjoying a hobby, and, yes, even working.

And think of the stress in your life that would be alleviated without rush-hour traffic! No more traffic jams, red lights, or crazy drivers. No more being late to work because of an accident or road construction. Home-business folks certainly aren't confined to their houses, but their "auto mobility" isn't mandated by morning and evening drive times.

4. *Reduced Stress and Less Office Protocol*

A demanding boss. Office politics. Expensive work clothes. These are among the things that prompt many traditional workers to yearn for the freedom of working from home. When you work for yourself at home, you're the boss. Some might laugh and say, "Yeah—and if you think that reduces stress, you're nuts!" They'd probably agree with a sign I saw recently that said, "The only thing more overrated than natural childbirth is the joy of owning your own business." Yes, it's true that being your own boss comes with its own set of stresses, but again the difference is control. You don't have anyone telling you when to attend staff meetings, file reports, or do paperwork. There is no annual review by the boss. There are no time clocks or procedures manuals. There is no corporate protocol other than what you determine.

Think about the things that might bug you about working for someone else: the amount you earn, the frequency with which you are paid, the benefits, the hours, office policies, the boss's personality, the company's philosophy or ethics. When you're the boss, you're in control of all these things and more. And, as studies find and as experience confirms, when we are in a position of greater control, our stress level is reduced. Besides, another major benefit of working for yourself (one which can lead to increased productivity) is the knowledge that you—not an employer—will enjoy the fruits of your labor.

Shaking the confines of an office also means dress-down day isn't limited to Friday. You're in control of what you wear! While it is just as important to convey a professional image when working from home as it is at the office, you decide what that means. If you want to get dressed up every day, that's great (especially if you deal with clients often), but if you're working all day with no one around but the kids, comfy clothes may be just right.

Now I realize that many home-business books tell you to get dressed each day just as if you were going to the office. I don't know about you, but I'd feel pretty silly sitting at home at my computer dressed in my suit, hose, and high heels with no one around but my children. Besides, one of my favorite perks of working at home is no more hasty pre-office stops at the "Git-It-N-Go" after ruining the last pair of pantyhose!

Another advantage of home-work is freedom from office protocol which, among other things, usually dictates a certain number of personal or sick days. For parents, that limit can mean stress. Once when I was working full-time and my firstborn was very young, I kept getting calls from the family daycare provider with whom she stayed. Three times in one month I had to leave work in the middle of the day to go pick up my marginally ill child. The daycare provider had no choice but to call me, and I had no choice but to go get my child. My employer didn't like those choices. On top of all that "working mother guilt," I also had to contend with nearly losing my job. That doesn't happen when you're your boss.

Many business owners, however, say that "being your own boss" is really a misnomer because your deadlines or customer demands become your boss. That can be true. I've certainly felt that way during some of my busiest seasons, but compared to the experience I just shared some things put the issue of being my own boss in perspective for me. Once while I worked, Allison, the second youngest of my five children, was staying the day with Debbie, who runs a Christian in-home daycare. This time when the phone rang for me to come pick up my not-so-marginally ill child, I didn't have to ask anyone's permission. I brought her home and held her on my lap while I edited a chapter. Later she lay sleeping under a blanket right near my desk while I faxed off my work. I remembered the conflict of many years before and smiled at the difference. Working from home definitely reduces stress, and it sure beats office protocol! Yes, at times the business may seem more like the boss than I, but I do like the ultimate control of being able to put my family first without asking anyone for permission.

5. *Increased Productivity*

When you have a home business, there is no idle chatter around the water cooler—unless you *want* to talk with the Sparkletts man when he drops off your new 10-gallon bottles. At home, you don't have to listen to the girl at the desk next to yours tell you how she lost her dog, wrecked her car, took her mother for surgery, and broke up with her boyfriend—all since she saw you at five o'clock last night. No more endless meetings dragging on, keeping you from accomplishing whatever the meeting is about. No more break-room gossip about Susie-So-and-So's latest affair to steal valuable minutes. Think of all the wasted time in an office environment! If you've been there, you know what I mean.

So it's no surprise that increases in productivity of at least 20 percent are common among home-based workers. In *Working from Home*, Paul and Sarah Edwards say, "With fewer interruptions, and the absence of office politics, people find their productivity goes up considerably. Electronic Services Unlimited's study of telecommuters reports that productivity gains of 40 to 50 percent are realistic."[6]

Gail found that out when she left her corporate office to do the same job from her home: "I get so much more done now. When I reviewed what I accomplished over a given period of time at corporate with what I did during the same amount of time working from home, I found significant gains. It's like putting a do-not-disturb sign on the door and telling your secretary to hold all calls. I don't have to answer anyone else's phone calls, and there's no idle chatter.

Now when I go in to their office and people stop to chat, I find myself thinking of what I need to do. It's so easy in an office to waste time, yours and your employer's. The drawback, of course, is that you're not in the social circle at work anymore, but that's my choice. I'd rather be closer to my child than my coworkers. That relationship is far more important."

6. *Personal Success*

For some people, success is based on their bottom line. For others, success is leaving a corporate office to hang out their own shingle. Some see success as being more available for their family because they work out of their home. For others, success means involving their children in their work, apprenticing a child, starting a ministry from home, or finding a way to integrate their faith with what they do. And many people find success in no longer merely contemplating their dreams, but instead following their heart and God's guidance and making those dreams happen.

Success in traditional work is often measured by the concrete specifics. How big is the paycheck? How favorable is the review? How'd you fare at promotion time? But for home-based workers, success often lies in the intangibles. Certainly we want to make money, but that is not the defining measure. So if you are considering this work option, spend some time defining what success is to you. Take this opportunity to pursue that "one thing" you've always wanted to do. As you read this book, research, study, and pray about this decision, ask the Lord to reveal to you the kind of success and goals He desires for you. After all, if we're pursuing God's plan for our lives, we'll find no greater success.

My Story

More family time, greater flexibility, no commute, reduced stress, less office protocol, increased productivity, and the opportunity to pursue success as I define it—I can identify with and appreciate all of these reasons for working from home, mainly because

I've experienced so many other ways of working. I've worked full-time outside the home, part-time outside the home, freelance, and at home for an employer before I began working at home for myself.

I have had to leave my child with another care provider from eight in the morning to six in the evening while I went off to work. I did that on days when my child wasn't sick, but just enough under the weather to make me worry. I did that on days when both of us would rather have stayed home and cuddled on the sofa with books and hot chocolate. I did that on days when my child tearfully cried, "Mommy, please don't go to work today"—and those were the days I cried the rest of the way to work.

As difficult as working full-time outside the home was, I liked doing what I did once I got to work. I understand why so many women enjoy climbing the corporate ladder. It can be fun up there! Sometimes it's nice to get a pat on the back for a job well done instead of a pat on the knee with a request for more juice. It's nice to feel intellectually stimulated and needed. It's nice to see the results of your efforts in a tangible and relatively immediate way. It's nice to talk with adults during the day. I do understand why many women love working, why it's often fun and rewarding, and how it's sometimes heart-wrenching as well. The bottom-line source of conflict for so many mothers is the need and/or desire to work versus the need and/or desire to have a certain quality home life. Home-based work can help ease that conflict. It certainly has for me.

Working from home has enabled me to both meet the economic needs of my family and find intellectual stimulation without putting those things above my family life. I am available to my family first. During some of my crunch times when I have to put in extra hours to meet deadlines and the laundry gets a bit behind, my family may not feel like they're first, but overall they are. Even during my busiest times, I am still more available to my family than I was when I worked full-time outside my home. The world may tell you that this is no way to run a successful business, but look what the world has done with the success of the family. (Besides, there's a lot more in the

Bible about succeeding in family life than in business life!) I definitely want a successful business, but not at the expense of things that have value for eternity.

I learned the importance of that when I was working in a high-stress, high-pressure job. I had a conversation one day with a man who told me something I'll never forget. He wisely said, "Don't sacrifice the permanent on the altar of the immediate"—and that's what I had been doing. The immediate was my job, and the permanent was my family. (That wise man is Tim Kimmel, and his book *Little House on the Freeway* is on my recommended reading list.) When he made that comment, I began to realize how—little by little—I had been letting certain immediacies take precedence over things that had permanent value.

So my home-business adventure began at my kitchen table one day when my husband said, "You know, considering what you're doing for your employer, you ought to start your own business." So I did. I started a desktop publishing business back when page-layout software was relatively new and in-house graphics capability wasn't so widespread.

Today, many years later, I still work from home, but in something completely different. I'm balancing my mothering with my other passion: my writing and speaking business. There were also a few years in between when I took a hiatus from my career and focused solely on my family. All along, the beautiful thing about being home-based has been the freedom to let my work adjust to the pace of my mothering, instead of running to keep pace with my career. Not everything I (or the many people profiled in this book) do is entirely *at* home. Speaking engagements, occasional broadcast work, and some interviews take me away from home periodically. Yet, I have found working primarily *from* home to be just what God ordered for our family. Perhaps you'll find the same thing. Now, let's look at what some others are doing from home as they make a living where they make their life.

2

Home Business Profiles

One of the most fascinating things about studying home businesses is meeting the unique people who run such a wide variety of enterprises. The home-based workforce has been called the fastest-growing economic sector in the United States. Learning what these folks are doing to earn money from home is not only interesting, but educational and often inspiring as well. You never know when someone else's story will give you that great idea you've been looking for, help you solve a problem, or spur your own creativity.

What follows are some personal stories of home-based workers across the country who are making a living and loving what they do. Why are they doing it? How are they doing it? What is the hardest thing they have to contend with? How has the Lord blessed them through their endeavors? They share their answers to these questions in the following stories.

ᘍ ᘍ ᘍ

Many years ago, I had the opportunity to record a broadcast about home-based employment on "Focus on the Family." Two dear friends joined me that day discussing their expertise in this field.

One of them was Posy Lough, a marketing maven who has run a successful home-based business for more than two decades.

Posy creates custom-designed counted cross stitch kits for sale in the gift shops and museum stores of America's historic sites. She preserves our country's story in stitches by combining her passion for American history with her love for business and family.

She began her career as a teacher and used her summers to begin her first home business. She'd always loved making crafts, so armed with talent and the help of her husband, Tom, she was able to sell some of her finished products in Williamsburg and even to Lord and Taylor's and Macy's! When her son came along, her business changed.

> *Tom and I had been married for 14 years and had given up on having a family, but God had other plans. When Kyser was born, we knew that we wanted me to be home to raise him. I knew I could continue the business I had in place, but something even better happened that changed the direction. I had been given the opportunity to redesign the counted cross stitch kit for Monticello, Thomas Jefferson's home. When my sister, Ceil Humphreys, came to take care of me when Kyser was born, we collaborated. I knew what the design should look like and with Ceil's talent to design cross stitch patterns, we created and sold that first kit.*

Now Posy has a highly successful wholesale business with more than 475 kits covering most major American historic sites including Mount Vernon, Grand Canyon, Mount Rushmore, and the Norman Rockwell Museum, as well as that first account, Monticello.

> *What makes this such a joy is that I love our country and its rich history. Every day is a new opportunity to learn more about our history and to develop a cross stitch product that adds to spreading the story of our country. After 20 years, I can honestly*

say that it is still as exciting as my first project. I contract with two independent designers who develop the cross-stitch charts, ten stitchers who complete the final cross stitch samples, and a fulfillment service that assembles the kits, which allows me the time for research, development, and marketing. I couldn't have succeeded without my husband's encouragement and help with the computer work , photography, and layouts.

Posy's best advice is to do what you love. When it doesn't feel like work, it's easy to stay motivated. Her favorite tip is to read, read, read! Make friends with the reference librarian at your public library. Everything you need to know to start up and run your home-based business is there, for free, including Internet resources.

The chance to be totally creative and my own boss cannot be equaled. I love pouring my life experiences and talents into my very own business. Kyser is now at Murray State University and lives in the dorm across town. Having a home business means that when he drops by, I still am an at-home mom! The perks are unbeatable.

Check out The Posy Collection at historic sites and the website: www.posycollection.com.

🌿 🌿 🌿

What if you feel the tug to begin ministry-related home-based work? Well this story's for you. The other woman on that "Focus on the Family" broadcast I mentioned was lifelong friend Brenda Koinis. She began her foray into working from home with a home-based muffin business, Cornerstone Cottage, which she began after her husband Steve discovered he had high cholesterol. She created the recipe for him and found a niche in the food market at the time.

Many MBA programs tell their students to plan an exit strategy when they begin businesses—quite a few businesses only operate for a season—by design—and many close with the owners calling them a success. At other times, a business leads to something the owner never initially envisioned. Such is the case with Brenda. She began a home-based business with muffins, but today she operates a home-based ministry called The H2O Project.

> *My favorite song is by Steven Curtis Chapman. It begins, "Saddle up your horses; we got a trail to blaze." It ends with, "This is the great adventure!" It defines my life. Saddle up. Go where God leads you. Enjoy the adventure. I learned to saddle up my horse through my muffin business. I had to be organized, delegate, stop worrying about the unexpected, ask questions, find answers, and convince others of a good idea. Now my trail has led to ministry where I still have to use all the skills I learned years ago. God never wastes anything—even though I never became the muffin magnate of my dreams, I am blazing the trails that He has chosen, and I am enjoying the adventure.*

The Koinis' home-based ministry journey began when she and her husband, Steve, watched a World Vision video that portrayed the desperate need for clean water in Ghana. She describes that day:

> *We saw footage of women and children who spend as many as seven hours every day carrying polluted water back to their families, and we watched as a boy who had ingested parasites had a full-grown guinea worm extracted from his leg. (We're talking three-feet-long here.) Then we heard this heart-rending statistic: Every eight seconds a child dies from the lack of clean water. Every eight seconds! That's four million lives lost every single year. Pick any disease that scares you. I assure you that*

only a fraction of four million people die from it each year. And this disease is 100 percent curable. These kids are drinking disease-infested surface water because they live in a village that doesn't have a clean water well. Our eyes were wet and our hearts were touched.

Fortunately, there are many fine organizations that stand ready to drill these much-needed wells. Unfortunately, they lack the funds they need in order to keep up with the demand. So God gave Brenda and Steve a vision to help—the H20 Project.

Many people feel like they've already given all that they can to the needy and are giving, rightfully so, to their churches and other charities. Without diminishing that, the solution that The H2O Project offers is this: What if, for just a couple of weeks, people gave up all beverages other than water—the stuff they really didn't need anyway, and maybe even were better off without? What if, for just 2 weeks, they saved up the money they were going to spend on themselves, for beverages, and spent it on someone else, for clean water wells?

There's a whole bunch of people out there buying sodas, juices, and rivers of coffee! Most people who give up these beverages for two weeks are able to contribute $10. "Third world math" is an amazing thing—that's enough, in most cases, to provide clean water for a whole lifetime to a child who right now is suffering from cholera and may not live another year.

Steve and I are asking church groups, school groups, civic groups, and individuals to take the H2O Challenge—to give up all beverages except water for two weeks, to save their drink money, and to contribute it to established well-drilling organizations, so that they can provide more water to those in desperate need. We've recently produced a video and completed a project-in-a-box format that will allow us to facilitate this simple service project all over the country. A group or individual can contact us via the Internet (thank goodness for modern technology!) and download virtually all that's needed to inform and encourage others to make this small sacrifice in order to save a life.

Brenda's favorite home-business advice is to stay on your knees, be organized, maintain your health, remember your priorities, and delegate. And if you feel the tug to work from home, perhaps instead of a business, God just might lead you to begin a ministry.

Check out The H20 Project at www.theh2oproject.org.

❧ ❧ ❧

Some home-business owners have found a way to combine for profit businesses with some ministry work. Like this woman.

In 1999 Renée-Ann Giggie started a small home-based business but didn't generate enough income to do only that so she worked outside the home as well. Lately she wants to leave the outside work environment for good and really get her business off the ground so she's investing a lot of time, energy, and money to do so.

The idea for this business started when looking for the perfect greeting card. They either have the right image on the cover, but the wording is not quite right, or vice versa. Thus began Cydrina's Cards & Labels®—personalized greetings for all occasions. I make business cards, address labels, wedding invitations, baby announcements, and lots more. The best part is that the customer gets to choose not only the wording but the image, the fonts, and colors. On your "Focus on the Family" broadcast about home employment, you said to use the gifts that God has given us. I am artistic so this business fits me well.

But Renée-Ann's business does more than just make a profit. She gives as well, through fund-raising she does for charity.

I have a lot of fun with the address labels because that's the fund-raising part of my business. For every sheet of labels sold, part of the cost goes to two nonprofit organizations that are dear to me. (After my husband recovered from a massive heart attack I began supporting one of the nonprofits—the Heart and Stroke Foundation.)

I now raise funds all year. I also held a special one-week fund-raising event for the two foundations. This was brought to the attention of a couple of radio stations in my town, and one of them did a radio interview. They focused on the two foundations, but mentioned my home business as well.

I know I have a long way to go yet. But I love what I do and my goal is not to get rich. As long as I have enough to help my husband with our bills and expenses, I am quite content. I love pleasing the customer too! I am not sure what God's plan is for me but one thing I know is this: He knows the desires of my heart (Psalm 37:4) and He does have a plan for me (Jeremiah 29:11).

Contact Renée-Ann Giggie, Cydrina's Cards & Labels® at cydrina@yahoo.com.

❧ ❧ ❧

An old television ad featured a woman wearing her pajamas and sitting in her home office. She talks about the advantages of working from home and describes a morning filled with faxes, e-mail, and tele-conferencing. She says, "I get tons done. I still haven't showered." Got the picture? Then meet Peg.

Peg Roen is a writer who worked for *Country America* magazine and then on staff for a major Christian publication company. While employed, Peg tested the waters first by freelancing after hours. She found that working at home was something she not only wanted to do, but could do. So she gave up a great job to work from home. Why? It may have had something to do with her pajamas.

"I've always loved pajamas!" Peg says. "I love working in them." Yet, like the TV ad, she gets "tons done." She's also quite professional (in spite of her morning work attire!). It's no wonder, then, that her favorite aspect of working from home is the professional and personal integration it allows. She describes it like this:

> *I start my day by making calls to the later eastern or central time zones. Then I put in a load of laundry and do dishes while they're all at lunch. I work out at a gym with my husband during my lunch, and in the afternoon I write. Sometimes I write in the evening, which means I can take time out in the afternoon to go grocery shopping while everyone else is at work. I don't feel the time pressures of being busy with work from 8 to 5. There's a lot more freedom.*
>
> *I also love having more time and energy to do small things for people, to give gifts of encouragement. When I worked at an office, I'd get home at 6 and be too tired to bake for anybody, or write a note, or even pick up the phone to call anyone. Now I can better integrate that into my day because my schedule is so much more flexible.*

For many home-based workers, isolation can be a problem. To combat that, Peg not only works out at a gym, but she also schedules meetings with editors over coffee. (She also finds, however, that she likes the time alone.) Another struggle that comes with being out of the traditional office with its more predictable pattern of work is choosing from among the vast number of options as to what you do and when you do it.

> *Sometimes I get real motivated with all I can do because there are so many avenues for writing, and I have so many ideas for selling what I write. However, if I do take time off (because I*

can decide when to work), I feel guilty because there's so much I could be doing. That can be incredibly frustrating. Once on a trip I took for a travel piece I did, I met a lot of other writers who inspired me. Afterward, I really struggled with the number of options I had. That was the moment I had to decide, "OK, what do I really want to do? What do I really like to write?" I have to feel good about what I do. So I took a hard look at what I do and prayed. I realized I am doing what I really want to do.

What advice can Peg offer?

If you can pour your heart into the things you're doing, it'll help you be content. And sometimes you compromise your grand wishes for seasons of your life. Keep in mind that those grand wishes could be in your future. I may never make the big time, but that's okay because I really enjoy what I'm doing.

❧ ❧ ❧

In 1987 Liz Curtis Higgs was working as a successful radio personality on a top-rated program and speaking 90 times a year. Her pregnancy, however, made her reconsider what she was doing. She didn't feel that she could continue doing both speaking and radio well while she was mothering, so she asked herself, "When I wake up every day, which of those things do I most want to be doing?" Since speaking was her passion and she'd accomplished her goals in radio, she chose to start her own full-time speaking business from her home office. Many of her Christian friends thought that leaving a "real job" that provided 75 percent of their family income and "real benefits" was crazy, but she said, "I just knew I had to be home with my wonderful child, and I knew I had to follow where God was leading, and that was speaking."

Not completely convinced she could make a living at her new endeavor, she nevertheless took a leap of faith. She also did her homework and joined the National Speakers Association. She knew enough people who were making a living speaking that she decided "if it can be done and if God is in it, then I'll be able to do it. If I'm on my own, then I'm in trouble."

She describes the beginning of her business: "My goal in the beginning was to be home with my children, which worked really well because nobody hired me! But gradually, word of mouth began to spread. Then after four years, the business hit critical mass—enough people heard me or about me, and word of mouth took over. All those early years of phone calling began to pay off." Her phone began to ring, and it hasn't stopped since.

Since 1986, Liz has spoken to 1500 audiences in all 50 states plus Germany, England, Canada, France, Ecuador, and Scotland.

After many years of doing 50, 80, 100 single presentations a year, Liz now speaks at just 20 weekend conferences a year, allowing more time for family and writing. Monday through Thursday she is in her upstairs writing office, working on her next novel. But she didn't begin as a novelist. As many home-based workers know, what we do often changes over the years.

When I was first published in 1993, I was primarily a speaker so my first seven nonfiction books were patterned after my presentations—lots of humorous or touching real-life stories, with a message of encouragement for women. Then, when my children became readers, I was compelled to write five children's books (lots of mothers have this urge, I've discovered!). The stories came so effortlessly, I can only credit God for their creation. As my children outgrew those books, so, it seems, did my calling to write more of them. In the late '90s, my hunger for God's Word continued to grow and I sensed a deeper calling in my work. Out of that came the Bad Girls of the Bible series— three books that combined fiction and nonfiction, storytelling and Bible study. Which brings us to fiction, the joy of my writer's heart.

Through all those years of radio, speaking, and writing nonfiction, my longing to write fiction continued to grow. In 1995 I joined a fiction writers group and began attending workshops, interviewing successful authors, and reading women's fiction by the pound. And writing. And plotting. And dreaming. Well. Here we are. Three novels, three short stories, and one novella so far. Sometimes dreams really do come true. May all the glory go to the Lord, who planted that dream inside me so long ago. For now, I'll be pouring my time and creative energy into writing more novels, simply because I believe a novel has the power to penetrate our hearts more quickly than a nonfiction book, and often at a deeper, more emotional level. Absolutely nothing I've done professionally—in broadcasting, speaking, or writing—has made my heart sing more than writing novels.

Liz's marriage partner is also her business partner. She's quick to say that Bill is the reason she's able to do what she does. Not only does he get the children to and from school and stay with them when Liz travels, but he also works full-time as director of operations in what Liz is quick to call "their" business. Bill worked for 15 years as a computer systems specialist and in Christian radio prior to their business.

Bill handles about everything but the actual speaking. He manages the money, takes phone requests for speaking engagements, and sets up my interview schedule, to name a few things. There's no way I could do what I do without Bill. A woman with children who longs after a speaking career has to have a supportive somebody in her life to make it happen.

Because of the volume of calls that Bill and Liz get each day, they have two business lines and a fax line apart from their residential phone. She's on one line and Bill's on the other during the day.

After-school hours usually find one or the other parent playing taxi driver for their two teenagers.

Where do they run this growing enterprise? In "the back 40," you might say—or rather "the back 2½." Liz started the business in a back bedroom: "I remember when I bought my first copy machine. I thought, 'I'm really an office now!'" Then when she felt she needed help in her business and it began to get harder to work with the children underfoot, she rented office space two blocks from home and hired two employees, one full-time and one part-time. Yet she had to begin speaking more to pay for the two salaries and office rent. After a year and a half of that, she and Bill decided, "This is really not smart." So they took the money they were putting into rent and bought a larger property with a separate building on it for their office. They now live on more than two-and-a-half acres and the office is in its own building right out the back door of their home, just the way they like it. Home is home and work is outside. "Now I don't drift into the office in the evening and suddenly find myself working," Liz says. "I can't recommend enough separating your home and your work."

What does she say about her success?

I think I'm exactly where God wants me to be. I don't think of it in terms of success. All of this is so much more than I could ever have hoped for, and I have to give the Lord all the glory for that. We pray hard, plan hard, and work hard, but it's God who blesses.

What advice does Liz have for home-based workers?

Physically separate your home and office. If I were putting an office in my house, I'd pay to put in an outside door and seal or block the inside door so that going to the office becomes an intentional act. It's so easy to work all the time, especially if you enjoy what you do. At the very least, close your door at the end of the day and put a "Closed" sign on it. Also, have office hours that you abide by so your family knows when they get you back. Then stick to them as best you can.

What does she like best about working from home?

The joy for me is working with my husband and being together a lot as a family. I think that's really important. When I started working from my home, my children were small, curled up at my feet like kittens. Now they are tall, talkative teenagers! And—this was the big surprise—they need more *from me, not less. Their needs are more complex, often involving emotional issues or important decisions that really require mom to be available. Writing more and speaking less, and doing that writing from home, have made these teen mothering years flow a lot more smoothly...so far!*

❧   ❧   ❧

Perhaps you feel God calling you to work at home, but He's asked you to wait. Maybe you've been waiting for a long time. God called Lori Raines to such a wait, but she now has a thriving business.

Years ago, I was a struggling young mother desperately wanting a home business so I could stay home and care for my child. I found the original edition of this book, Working at Home, *and read it cover to cover, making highlights and notes in the margins. Somehow it was lost, and my goal had to be shelved because I had a husband who didn't support me, and I could not find anything I could do at home. Then in 1996, I bought a book on calligraphy and a set of pens, and set out to learn this time-honored craft. In 2001, I began Calligraphy by Lori. Today, I have a proud, supportive husband, a beautiful* teenage daughter, and a thriving home business as a much-in-demand calligrapher, working with brides all over the country and around the world.

Since Lori had to wait to see God accomplish this, she offers this advice.

I think the most important thing for anyone wanting to work at home is to realize that God's timing is of utmost importance. I tried several things in the past in the hopes of staying at home, but lacked the maturity to handle such responsibility, and did not have the support system I needed. I was just barking up the wrong tree then. I don't have the personality to sell children's toys, but I do have the creative gifts and personality to be a calligrapher, which I love. However, God used the last seven years to hone that skill and bring out my gift to where I could work at home doing this. As I grew older and circumstances in my life changed, the Lord knew that now I was ready for such a challenge and blessing!

The advantages of working at home are plentiful. Lori loves the timing of this business in her life to meet the current needs of her family.

I also see that being home-employed now is the right time for me since I have a daughter. I can play a big part in her life during her teenage years, and I can be at home to greet her when she comes home. Now, more than ever before, children need their moms at home! I have the freedom to put the pen down and be there for my daughter—to talk, hug, and encourage her, to be there when she needs me. And it also takes the sole financial burden off my husband.

God knew my desires and knew I could be such a huge blessing to my husband and my daughter by being at home, being able to keep the home the way I wanted—free of mom flying into the house fried out of her mind after working all day, throwing dinner together, and going to bed exhausted—missing out on important time as a wife and mother!

I never forgot your words, Lindsey. A new copy of your book sits on my shelf above my desk, dog-eared and highlighted, and I never completely gave up on my dream. You were the first person to introduce me to the possibility of this life I lead and I thank you. Please know your words to me early on have had a profound effect on me and my thriving business. It's the first book I recommend whenever I know someone wanting the blessing of working at home.

You can contact Lori Raines, Calligraphy by Lori at calligraphybyLori@yahoo.com.

❧ ❧ ❧

If you work at home now or are considering starting your own home business, be on the lookout for similar success stories. They're everywhere. Look for them in your reading, when you talk with vendors, through your networking contacts, everywhere you go. Being interested in others and what they are doing can be very inspiring. We can learn so much from one another.

3

Making
the Decision

Are you still trying to make the decision to work at home? Deciding to start my business wasn't easy. But, perhaps like you, I wanted to use the gifts the Lord had blessed me with and we needed the income.

My desire for a home business started when my first child was three months old. I was at home all day with my wonderful new baby daughter. I loved being a mom and felt like I was adjusting to motherhood quite well.

I knew, however, that with the new baby it would be tough for me to get back into my pre-pregnancy job of television news. My degree was in broadcast communications and I had a passion for the business.

One of my dear Christian high-school friends and college roommates was also a "journalism junkie." We made a pact in our sophomore year of high school: "Never get married before 25 and never have kids (unless you hire a nanny)!" Now I was far from being an unchurched heathen, but I had a drive to get things accomplished in my career. I was also influenced by the ever-growing antifamily, pro-career society that was especially vocal on the college campus.

Before we earned our degrees, that roommate broke our pact by getting married. I was first to break the other clause when I had my first child early in my marriage (without the nanny). The whole point of this is that God plants desires and abilities in us and changes hearts for specific purposes.

While I was pregnant I began to feel convicted to stay home with my baby, even though I still wanted to use my gifts for the Lord. I began to pray and read Christian books promoting strong traditional families, motherhood, and being a godly woman. God changed my desire for being the next Dianne Sawyer to that of being a stay-at-home mom. What He didn't take away were some of the abilities, talents, and motivation He had created within me.

I struggled with guilt over having "ambition." I just didn't know what to do with it! I loved my new role as wife and mother, was blessed with a strong Christian husband, and was growing in the Lord. Yet there were days when mild frustration would rear its ugly head. For example, an especially exciting news story would break and I'd think how much fun it would be to cover it; my college friend would call and tell me about her latest reporter stint at XYZ-TV; or I would read an author bio at the end of an article describing her "blissful" life as a mother and freelance writer.

But I snapped back to reality quickly when I thought of getting back into the grind of a job now that I had this wonderful child. My husband tried his best to understand how I could be so dedicated to being home with our new baby yet experience occasional and intense frustration as well.

Struggling with the desire to use some of the gifts God has given me was just one factor leading to the idea of having a home business. The other was more mundane—money. We really wanted to have a traditional one-income family, but it's tough at times to make it on one income in a two-income society!

Getting a full-time job seemed like a logical answer. I could deal with that "ambition thing" and bring in an income alongside my hardworking husband. But when I began to seriously think about it, I got knots in my stomach and tears in my eyes. I really did want to be home!

So what's a mother to do? I had reached the state of desperately wanting to make money at home, but didn't have the foggiest idea of how to go about it. I had moderate sewing ability and tried making baby quilts. I made a grand total of two! I wanted to write, but I didn't really have anything to write about then that I thought other people would want to read. I tried several other options and managed to contribute enough to get by financially without getting a full-time job for awhile, but I didn't have a clue about anything even remotely resembling a home business. As I mentioned in chapter 1, I tried out quite a few different working situations in order to meet our financial obligations, but I never quit praying for a way to make money at home. Several years later the Lord answered my prayer.

Waiting was the Lord's plan for me. Although it was difficult for me to see at the time, the different income-producing options in my life as well as all the time at home served to get me to the place where the Lord wanted me before He answered my prayer. I was learning, growing, and developing what some call "hidden art." (More on this in a moment when we discuss your calling.)

So where do you begin? Do you want to earn an income from home, but are unsure where to start? Try starting with this little quiz:

1. Do I feel the Lord's direction to do this?

2. What is my calling and what are my passions?

3. What would I enjoy doing and what are my gifts, talents, and experiences?

4. Does my spouse agree with my decision?

5. Would my family be supportive?

6. Am I suited for working at home?

7. Is there a market for what I want to do?

8. Have I researched my topic?

1. *Do You Feel the Lord's Direction?*

When you're trying to decide whether to start a home business, the best place to begin is on your knees.

Before tackling something as important as a home enterprise, spend time with the Lord. Be confident that He is leading you in that direction and that you are considering this option for the right reasons. Deuteronomy 28:2 says that if we are obedient to the Lord He will bless us. Yet how can we be obedient if we do not know His plan for us? How can we know His plan if we are not seeking Him? We must spend time daily in prayer and in God's Word. If you have had trouble in this area of your life, begin now to discipline yourself to spend time with God. A high percentage of small businesses close within the first five years. In light of this fact, be sure you are in the Lord's will and are following His guidance with each step of the decision-making process.

2. *What Is Your Calling and Passion?*

Many business books tell you to start by evaluating your skills and talents, but if you stop there and miss identifying the area where you feel called to serve, you might miss your best option. Some people say they are driven; others say they are called. Decide if you are in either category.

Sometimes it may take awhile to learn what God has in mind for you. Or perhaps the Lord has been cultivating you for a home business in the things you have been doing up till now. The point is to be alert to what God is doing in your life. Some people know very distinctly that they are called to a specific task, while others may have an idea but don't know how to implement that idea into a home business.

To find the business that fits your calling, ask yourself these questions: What excites me? What things or issues bother me? What things am I passionate about? Author Mary Pride also suggests asking: "What is burning inside me? What do I want to change or improve? What drives me crazy? You see, the reasons you are wondering why everyone else is so selfish/ignorant/apathetic or whatever about the issue burning in your heart is that God has given this issue to you, not to them.'"[1] Don't complain; get to work! Brainstorm about solutions to the problems that bug you and ask the Lord to give you wisdom.

If you hate the selection of children's clothing in your town and have the talent, start a line of your own. If you love working with the elderly and hate to see them lonely or in need of a caregiver, start a referral service for live-in or part-time help. If your sole motivation is to make money, you have probably made a poor business choice. Instead, if you have a passion for the business you have chosen, the work will have more meaning to you. If you get all excited about a particular issue, try to make that issue a part of your business.

Mary Pride also says that by doing the humble things in life with zest and unto the Lord, you cultivate skills for your business and you give God an opportunity to open doors for you. This can be called "hidden art," as Edith Schaeffer describes in her book *The Hidden Art of Homemaking*. Mary says, "The point is that while you are trying to become excellent at everything you do, one of your tasks will emerge as your calling."[2]

During the period of time when I began to pray for a home business and the time I actually started one, the Lord gave me many opportunities to develop hidden art in my life. At one point prior to my home business I was working for a Christian advertising agency. I got to do some writing, but primarily I worked on a computer. I had never touched a computer before that time, and I didn't relish the idea of touching one then. I would have told anyone that I did not have the temperament or inclination for such machines. I have to call my husband if the can opener won't work and am basically allergic to anything with an on-switch.

However, the training and experience I got there was the starting point of my home business a short time later. I also began to write as much as I could. I wrote in my journal and volunteered for writing assignments at church and for my employer. The Lord was also teaching me on the home front. I was learning much in the repetitive things of life such as housework, child-rearing, and organizational skills. Even though I didn't know it at the time, He was developing "hidden art" within me and helping me see how I could put my calling into action. Working on a computer in an office was a humbling task for me. Doing the dishes, disciplining the kids when they needed it, and learning how to be organized wasn't (and isn't) always fun either, but the Lord used those disciplines to open a door to my own home business.

Now, desktop publishing wasn't my passion in life, but I was passionately motivated to do it. Working from home so I could be with my children more was the desire of my heart. I didn't feel particularly called to design printed materials on a computer (although I enjoyed it), but I did feel called to be home with my children. Today, my home-based work more closely reflects my calling and my passion. I know that God has prepared, gifted, enabled, and called me to the work I do, and I love it. And that is a tremendous blessing.

As you set about making the decision to work from home, prayerfully consider your calling. Seriously evaluate the things you feel passionately about. Ask God to lead you to a business that reflects these things. Working in any old money-making job can be draining, but working in the arena of our calling and passions is energizing. We can then find great meaning and value in what we do; we find significance that extends far beyond the task at hand.

3. *What Are You Good At?*

After you have put much prayer and thought into your calling, list all of your interests, hobbies, and talents. Sometimes identifying your calling brings to mind an obvious home business choice. If it doesn't, sit down with paper and pen and write down all the things that you really enjoy doing. If you don't like what you're doing, there is no point in making a business out of it. Then write down all the gifts you feel the Lord has blessed you with. (Don't say you don't have any gifts; everyone has at least one!) Write down all your talents.

Then list all your experiences and training—paid, volunteer, or on the home front. Starting a business in which you have no experience can be dangerous.

Perhaps you feel called to work with children, or do ministry work, or help the elderly, or write, but a business doesn't just spring to mind. Go to the lists you just made. If your calling is working with children and one of your gifts is teaching, you could start a family childcare center or teach kids gymnastics, piano, or anything else that might be on your talent list. If you have a heart for the elderly (your calling), you like to shop (your interest), and you are good at details and organization (your gift), you might want to start a shopping service for the elderly. Get the picture?

This selection process may be elementary for the person who distinctly knows what the Lord is leading him or her to do. If you are such a person, just count your blessings and skip this chapter! But many other people struggle with exactly what they can do. If you are one of these, don't despair. Go prayerfully before the Lord, then organize your calling, interests, gifts, talents, and experiences on paper, and continue to pray. You'll be surprised by how much clearer you can think when your thoughts are written down.

Also, don't overlook your hobbies. Many people's pastimes have turned into thriving businesses. One Alabama woman turned her hobby into a full-time enterprise when her pig folk-dolls were noticed by a woman who had worked with Xavier Roberts of Cabbage Patch® fame. That lady suggested that she copyright the design of her dolls. She did so, and soon customer orders were coming in faster than she could fill them.

If you love to make crafts in your spare time, consider an arts-and-crafts business. If you love woodworking, try your hand at it for profit. If you are a "fixer-upper" and like people and old houses, look into operating a bed-and-breakfast enterprise. The point is to choose something that you would like to do and feel you would be good at.

4. *Does Your Spouse Agree?*

If you are married, make sure your spouse is in full agreement with your decision to begin a home business. Home-business owner Judy Johannesen wrote me about how her husband hated the particular product she was selling and discouraged her efforts. When she found something else she could do from home that she would like better and when she had her husband's full support, everything changed. He even became an integral part of the business. "After a couple of years home with my children, I got itchy feet and tried my hand at selling part-time, working around the kids' schedules. It was there that I learned record-keeping and business tax information. However, my husband was not in agreement with me.

"Fortunately, I also took a calligraphy class, and this hobby has developed into a full-fledged business. The best part is that I have the wholehearted support and encouragement of my husband. He's given me lots of marketing ideas, shares a workspace in his shop, and helps in the production. He has also built me a beautiful lettering area, mailroom, and storage space. The Lord has really blessed me with Bob, the kids, and this business, and I pray that He blesses the lives of those my work touches."

Judy's business began to prosper after she adapted her work to God's leading and had the support of her husband. If your house is divided, you will not experience peace in your marriage or success in your business.

5. *Does Your Family Support You?*

The whole family doesn't have to share your enthusiasm, but it is vital that they *support* you in your enthusiasm and help keep the domestic train on track. One person cannot run a home business and remain chief cook, bottlewasher, maid, and chauffeur and still keep his or her sanity and health.

It is much easier to withstand the difficulties and demands of a home business if your family is behind you 100 percent. If the kids expect Mom to never miss a beat in seeing to their needs and don't offer encouragement and help in her business endeavors, it's time to do one of three things: Get new kids, throw out the idea of a home business, or involve your children in your work by enlisting their help and support. Since the first two ideas aren't so hot, try working with your kids. If they're older and really hate what you're doing, listen to them. They may have valid concerns and could suggest some alternatives to the things about your business that are bothering them. Listen to complaints such as "Mom, we miss you. You seem upset a lot since you began putting 50 hours a week in the business." But complaints like "Mom, I don't like your business because the trash is always overflowing and there aren't any clean glasses" should be dealt with as well. Swiftly lead your children to the trash can as you hand them a garbage bag and direct them to the dishwasher for front-line involvement in the domestic battle!

Working at home is a wonderful opportunity to teach your children about the value of a job well done, a good work ethic, cooperation, family togetherness, and, of course, business skills. All too many children have no idea what Mom and Dad actually do when they are "at work." Working at home lets them not only see what it is that Mom or Dad does, but allows them to get involved and learn as well. (More tips on involving your children in a later chapter.)

6. *Are You Suited for Working at Home?*

Determine if the lifestyle is really for you. If you are a highly structured person who likes a rigid routine, lots of people around, direction from others, and supervision, then working at home may not be for you.

A *Birmingham News* article reported, "Several studies of successful entrepreneurs indicate that they are well-disciplined toward their work, usually are highly competitive, creative, careful about money, have relatives who were entrepreneurs, and often began making money at an early age."[3] The book *In Business for Yourself* lists several characteristics that lead to entrepreneurial success: knowledge of the business you are undertaking; drive, energy, and commitment; persistence; self-confidence; goal-setting; risk-taking; and the use of feedback and outside resources.[4] If you abound in one or more categories and you are convinced that you are being led by the Lord to undertake your enterprise, don't let deficiencies in the other categories stifle your dream.

Take inventory of your personality with this "suitability quiz":

- Do you have the organizational abilities and patience to balance a home and a business under one roof, particularly if you have children?
- Are you highly motivated?
- Are you a self-starter?
- Do you set high standards for yourself, or do you perform better when you have outside direction?
- Do you need structure in your life, or do you like a lot of freedom?
- Are you goal-oriented?
- Do you gain pleasure from seeing your goals accomplished, or are you a procrastinator?
- Can you set and meet your own deadlines?
- Do you enjoy being in your home?
- Do you have adequate space for your work?
- Do you need other people around for social interaction?
- Do you need an exciting environment with hustle and bustle to keep you interested?
- Do you adapt easily, or are you a "rigid" person?

Being objective about yourself can be difficult. Carefully consider each question. If you have trouble answering any of the questions, try talking with your spouse, a close friend, or your parents. Ask them how they would answer the questions about you. You may see yourself as a self-starter, but your spouse may see you as a procrastinator. You may not feel like you are patient or well-organized, but perhaps a friend who knows you very well can show you ways that you are.

Working at home will be easier and more productive if you have the right temperament. It helps to be motivated, organized, independent, goal-oriented, and flexible. If you are a chronic procrastinator who is not particularly motivated or enthusiastic and needs a lot of people around, then you will probably experience difficulty and frustration in working at home.

7. *Is There a Market for What You Want to Do?*

Make sure there is a market for your product or service. Determine how your product or service is different from what might already be available. How does your product or service help your customers or clients? How is it unique? You need to know—and be able to verbalize—why your product or service is worth paying for. Who would most want to purchase what you have to offer? If you answer "everyone," then you have not done enough market research. Find out as much as you can about the people who need your service or product. You must know who they are and where they are in order to let them know you have something they need. You also need to know how you can reach them. Direct mail? Cold calls? Magazine ads? The way to reach your market varies according to who and where your market is.

Success doesn't depend on being entirely original. In fact, it's difficult in today's market to be truly original. But finding your niche is important. For example, if you live in a college town and love doing technical typing with statistics and charts, you may have a niche in the word processing market there. Since most people hate that sort of typing, you may have a head start if you see that niche and advertise yourself effectively. Instead of promoting yourself as a general typing service, you might advertise yourself as a technical word processing service, perhaps even offering pickup and delivery. This further distinguishes you from the competition.

Big business invests large amounts of start-up capital in market research to actually determine the need for the business. Many small business advisers recommend this as well, but most people beginning home businesses do not have a great deal of money to invest in this area. Market research doesn't have to be done on a large scale by a professional market research firm costing big bucks. Perhaps you could approach it like Edith Flowers Kilgo did. The author of *Money in the Cookie Jar,* Edith describes how she decided to start selling handmade dolls. Before she began, she did some market research that cost her virtually nothing. She made a model of the doll she wanted to produce (noting the production time and costs) and let her four-year-old daughter run it through the mill (the quality-endurance test). She found several problems and fixed them before ever making a second doll. Next she began to listen to all the comments from people who saw the doll that her daughter carried everywhere. She got a feel for how people felt about the dolls and what they would be willing to pay for them. She gave them as gifts and gained further insight into marketing her craft from the mothers' comments. Through this simplified test of her market she learned about her product's durability, salability, and profit potential before ever beginning production.[5]

Your market research might be as simple as a browse through the Yellow Pages. If you want to start a secretarial service and there are already a large number of them listed in your small-town phone book, maybe you should consider an alternative choice. The old adage is absolutely true: For a successful business, find a need and fill it. Just make sure there really is a need.

8. *Have You Researched Your Business Decision?*

After you have decided what you want to do (or at least have narrowed it down), research your choice. Learn all you can about home businesses. Spend some time in the library, bookstore, or online and learn all you can about what you are going to do. (See chapter 4 for more ideas.) Read as many books, periodicals, and reference sources as you can about your subject.

When I got serious about my writing, I knew I had a lot to learn. Simply stringing sentences together at the word processor does not make one a published author. I began to research the publishing field, which was very different from my newswriting background. Attending writing seminars and interviewing other authors provided "inside information." What I learned (and am continuing to learn) about the field has helped me a great deal.

If you want to start a secretarial or word-processing business, check out library books on such services. If your library doesn't have any listings, check *Books in Print* for titles and get a copy through interlibrary loan or visit your local bookstore. If you want to sell your handmade crafts or start a home-based business of any kind, research all you can about all the aspects of your particular business. Research the product or service itself as well as all the aspects of running a business, marketing, and any other areas in which you need instruction.

Check your local community college or city recreation department for continuing-education courses or noncredit courses related to your field. Many times these classes are available at a nominal fee and cover small-business basics as well as specific instruction in a great number of fields. We do not have to embark on anything inadequately informed; that would be sheer folly in today's information age. There are enough resources at hand to equip and prepare you for your endeavor and to save you from many wrong turns down the road.

Above all, you must be dedicated to your reason for working at home. It has been said that productivity is the by-product of motivation and attitude. You need both the reasons for wanting to accomplish your goal and the attitude necessary to make the reasons work. If your reason for working at home is six months old and cooing in the crib and you are fiercely dedicated to being the significant caregiver, you have a head start on success because your motivation is so strong. If your only reason to work at home is for extra money, then when the going gets tough you may opt to throw in the towel or go the conventional "outside job" route.

4

Home Business
Ideas

I f you're still trying to decide what work you could do from home this chapter might help trigger an idea. The best ideas for a home business come from your own personal list of interests, skills, gifts, hobbies, experiences, and "things that bug you." Some of the best businesses to start from home are service businesses because they usually require less start-up capital, they tend to have little to no inventory, and a profit is often realized sooner. The type of business you choose, whether *at* home most of the time or *from* home with some of the work done away from your home office, depends on your age, your mobility, whether or not you have children, their ages, if you have supplemental childcare, and how much you want to be away from your home. Some of the ideas listed in this chapter are included because the base of such operations could be at home. Some refer to out-of-home businesses that could be adapted to a home business.

This list is just the tip of the iceberg. Ideas for home businesses are all around you. Look in the index of the Yellow Pages, in advertising that you read in newspapers and magazines, in ads you hear on radio and television, and in conversation with other people. Look for ways to adapt a unique idea or a "traditional job" into a home business. If you are looking for a way to work at home, perhaps this list can trigger a potential business idea for you.

Animals

Animal breeding
Dog obedience training
Horseback riding instruction
Pet hotel

Pet grooming service
Pet sitting
Portable petting zoo

Computer-Oriented Businesses

Computer consulting service
Computer repair service
Computer training (children or
  adults)
Data processor

Desktop publishing
Graphic design
Information broker
Research service
Software creator

Art & Craft Businesses

Alterations
Appliqué
Art broker
Art show promoting
Calligraphy
Cartooning
Ceramics
Commercial art
Craft businesses
Custom pattern business
Doll making
Drapery making
Flower arranging
Frame making

Furniture making/restoring
Glass etchings
Handicrafts co-op gallery
Jewelry making
Leatherwork
Painting
Pillows
Quilts
Sewing
Soft sculpture
Stained glass
Stenciling
Wall hangings
Woodworking

Employment Services

Career counseling
Employment agency
Employment for the elderly
Executive recruiting service

Résumé writing & career
  counseling
Temporary-help service

Food

Bakery
Candy making
Catering
Cookbook author
Cooking course

Custom cakes
Health food/product sales
Nutrition consultant
Specialty food sales

Personal Services

Bridal veil designer
Cosmetics
Fitness trainer
Hair salon
Home organization
Image consulting
Nail salon

Personal shopping service
Professional organizer
Teaching (art, music, aerobics…)
Tutoring
Wedding consultant
Wedding photography
Make-up artist

Publishing and Writing Businesses

Advertising copywriter
Christian consumer directory
Desktop publishing
Freelance writing
Local cookbook publishing

Newsletter publishing
Parents' directory
Rental list publishing
Technical writing

Recreation and Entertainment Businesses

Balloon delivery service
Entertainment agent
Party planning

Travel buddies (for single or elderly people)
Vacation planning
Video production company

Services to Business

Accounting
Advertising agency
Advertising, specialty
Bartering club
Bookkeeping
Business brokerage
Clipping service
Collection agency
Consulting business
Coupon mailer service
Data processing
Delivery services
Drafting
Graphic Design

Information broker
Janitorial services
Medical transcriptionist
Plant rental services
Public relations agency
Publicist
Secretarial/word-processing service
Telephone answering service
Temporary service (specialized)
Typesetting service
Website designer
Window-washing service

Services to the Home

Architect
Cleaning service
Closet customizing
Errand service
Firewood sales
House painting
House sitting/in-home care
Interior designer
Ironing
Kitchen remodeling
Landscape design

Lawn-care service
Maid service
Pest control
Photography
Plant care
Pool cleaning & repair
Shopping service
Upholstery
Window treatments
Window-washing service

Service Businesses, Miscellaneous

Budget interior design
Childcare service
Event planning service
Gift basket service
Nanny agency
Personalizing items
Printing

Private investigator
Reading improvement service
Reunion planner
Scholarship search service
Telephone wake-up service
Travel agency

Miscellaneous Businesses

Antique restoration
Auto wholesaling, customizing, or repair
Bed & breakfast inn
Burglar alarm sales/installation
Buying foreclosures
Engraving
Fashion design
Flea market & swap meet promoting
Herb farming
Import/export

Investment counselor
Mail-order business
Music therapist
Party plan companies
Physical therapist
Public speaking
Real estate
Real estate investment guide
Rubber stamp business
Security consultant
Seminar promoting
Speech therapist

Direct Sales Companies

Many women are finding the benefits of having their own home-based business—and avoiding the difficulty of an entrepreneurial start-up—by working for an established company in direct sales. Special skills are usually not necessary and the companies often provide marketing support and ideas, training, and start-up kits. Some of these companies at the time of this writing are:

Avon
Beauty Control Cosmetics

Creative Memories
Discovery Toys
Home Interiors & Gifts
Longaberger Baskets
Mary Kay Cosmetics
Multiples at Home
Shaklee
The Carlisle Collection
Tupperware
Weekender Casual Wear

And there are many others.

Setting Up Your Business

S ome people are confident that they are cut out for a home business or that they are following the Lord's clear leading as to what that business should be. But they may struggle with the next step: "How do I get from *wanting* a home business to *having* one?"

Start-up doesn't have to be a scary thing, contrary to what you may have read. As you delve into setting up your own business, you will discover a mass of new information. Even if you think you can remember everything you read and hear, write it down! Keep copious notes on everything you find out, think about, and do in the beginning. You may not think you will need all this information, but down the road that bit of information might be just the thing you're looking for. Start keeping organized notes when you begin gathering information and continue throughout your start-up. Later you will be glad you did. Here is a checklist to help you begin setting up your business.

1. Determine the amount of time you want to devote to the business.

2. Estimate your start-up costs.

3. Determine the amount of money available for start-up costs.

4. From your start-up list, determine your initial priorities.

5. Obtain the proper identifying numbers and licenses; research federal, state, and local requirements.

6. Determine your legal form.

7. Choose your name and register it.

8. Open a business account.

9. Have your printing done.

10. Determine your record-keeping system.

11. Establish a business plan.

12. Get your initial equipment and supplies.

13. Decide where in your house you will locate your business.

14. Get organized.

1. *Determine the amount of time.*

Estimate the time you think it will take to get your business going and to operate it successfully. Make sure you can invest the time to get your business off the ground. If you begin blindly, without any thought as to how much time your endeavor will take (planning instead to deal with things as they come along), you are setting yourself up for frustration, if not failure. If you have children, decide at the onset the number of hours each week that you are willing to put your child in substitute care if necessary.

Don't let yourself get into this situation: You embark on what you hope will be a successful business, knowing that it will take a lot of your time but not actually estimating the amount of time you realistically have available. You realize the mess you are in when everything in your home and business needs your attention at the same time and your daily 24 hours look hopelessly inadequate. You are overworked and unhappy. You want business success, but not at the expense of your family. The problem: You didn't evaluate your schedule and the priorities that affect the number of hours you have to accomplish "X" in a given day, so you are going nuts trying to work full-time at everything. (See chapters 10 through 12 for a more detailed look on how to find the time to manage your home and business.)

2. *Estimate your start-up and monthly costs.*

Make a list of what you will need and what it should cost to get your business open. (Some advisers say to double that figure.) It may take three times longer than most people think to reach their expected level of revenue in a new business. First-year expenses are usually twice as much as expected.[1] Do not just guess what it will cost you to set up; let your fingers do the walking through your phone book and save yourself some time and energy in estimating your costs.

What are some of the things you need? Consider equipment and supplies: office furniture, a telephone listing or separate line, office supplies, inventory (if product-related), letterhead, envelopes, business cards, licenses and fees, printed business checks, legal and professional fees, and initial advertising. Check around the house before you purchase anything; use what you already have. You will usually find that many items on your list, from paper clips and notepaper to an office chair, can be confiscated from somewhere in your house.

Estimate your monthly expenses as well. You'll be surprised how fast your second month in business rolls around requiring financial support often before your profit has appeared. Some items require capital only in the start-up phase (such as a telephone business line or office furniture). You also need to know how much money it will take to keep you in business three weeks after you open your doors, four weeks after that, and so on. These items include your telephone bill, supplies (particularly if you are product-oriented), advertising, and anything else that you will need on a monthly basis in order to operate.

3. *Determine the amount of money available for start-up costs.*

After you know how much money you will need to get started, decide where the money will come from: personal savings, family contributions, personal bank loans, small business loans, investors. Will you need a lot of start-up capital or a little? Will you need a loan? Can you use part of your savings? Some businesses can begin on a shoestring and require little more than sweat of the brow to get going. (Great way to start!) Others take considerable financial investments to begin. If yours is one of the latter type, your best bet would be to wait until you have the amount of start-up capital you need on your own or reevaluate your business choice.

The best way to begin a home business (especially for people with little or inadequate business training) is to begin small. Start out small and manageable and plan to grow. Don't plan to begin big and then end up with nothing but giant debts and a broken business.

In *Homemade Money*, Barbara Brabec says, "Few individuals are able to get a bank loan at the start of their home business, either because they lack start-up capital or the kind of collateral the bank requires, or they're simply reluctant to pledge to the bank what collateral they do have, usually savings accounts, equity in a home, or cash surrender value of an insurance policy. In the end, many people decide that it's easier to borrow from their own savings account, or perhaps a relative. Others simply figure out how to raise their own venture capital through a variety of entrepreneurial activities."[2]

The Small Business Administration (SBA) offers many financing programs, but this organization doesn't make direct loans to an individual or company. It primarily guarantees business loans made by local banks and other lenders to small-business clients. The agency guarantees up to 85 percent of the value of the loan balance. The maximum loan size is $2 million and the maximum guaranteed amount is $1 million, although they average about $164,000. The SBA says some of the reasons loan requests are turned down is lack of experience of the small-business client, insufficient cash flow to repay the loan, and insufficient owner equity in the business.

If you feel you need a loan to get started, visit your local bank with a well-written business plan. (More details on business plans later in the chapter.) This will greatly enhance your chances. Submit this to your bank. If you are turned down, ask for an SBA loan guarantee. The bank, if interested, will then contact the SBA directly. Do not rush into any financial decisions. If you can start your business without a loan, you will be much better off.

Make sure you weigh the costs before you start. Statistics show that the main reason small businesses fail is lack of sufficient capital. Yet if your capital is limited (isn't everyone's?), don't let that stop you; just be realistic in the financial planning of your endeavor by starting small.

4. *Determine your initial priorities.*

Look at your start-up list and decide what is absolutely essential to get your business going. Don't buy anything that is not necessary in the beginning. At first glance you may feel everything on your list is vital, but after looking at the bottom-line figure of what it will cost you to purchase everything on that list at once, you will probably find a way to prioritize those items. For example, if your business is computer-based and you need specific equipment to operate, figure out exactly what you will be doing the first month. You may find that you can get by without some of the equipment you need until a little later down the road. You may have to bite the bullet by not having all the equipment you need in the beginning in exchange for a more comfortable cash-flow position, which is vital to your start-up survival. Be thrifty in what you do have to buy. How many widgets will you have to sell, or how long will you have to work, to pay for your purchase?

For example, when I began my company, I started out with one Macintosh computer. It was almost the bottom of the line in quality, but it got the job done. Later I upgraded the memory in that machine and even later sold that computer and bought a more powerful one. I gradually added more equipment as I could afford it, procuring some of it through bartering and client financing. I certainly didn't have everything I needed in the beginning, but neither did I have a wealth of start-up capital. I suffered through endless disk-swapping until I could really afford a hard drive (hard drives were not internally installed as they are today). I used a friend's laser printer until I could get my own. It took awhile to get all the equipment that I have now, but financially it was the only way possible without racking up tens of thousands of dollars in debt before I opened my doors for business. Had I tried to purchase everything on my start-up list in the beginning, I probably would never have gone into business at all.

If your company produces something tangible to sell, you can probably think of a great deal of things you need to create your product, speed up production, and make your work easier. Just be alert to the things on that list that are necessary for you to open your doors and the things that can wait. Many things may seem vital in the beginning, but careful evaluation, prioritizing, and a little creativity will reveal what is really essential for start-up and what can wait a month, three months, or a year.

5. *Obtain the proper identifying numbers and licenses; research federal, state, and local requirements.*

Check your local, county, and state agencies for all fees and licenses that you must legally obtain in order to set up shop. Check with the Department of Commerce in your state. This agency may be able to help you locate other specific agencies that you need to contact for your business. A "Permit to Do Business" is often required. Also check zoning restrictions for your business. Both of these can usually be done by contacting the city planning or zoning department or your homeowners association. One of the most-asked questions about home businesses is "But are they legal?" The answer is probably yes, but check with the city planning department in your area. If you are handling food, your business is probably regulated by the county health department, and regulations are usually more prohibitive. Zoning laws are set by each municipality. A good rule of thumb is that, if you do not have an excessive number of clients coming to your door, the UPS or Federal Express man doesn't make daily stops at your home, and you don't have the street blocked or use loud machinery, you are probably okay. However, don't leave anything to chance. Find out if your particular home business is legal in your area before you start it. For example, one man employed several people in his home business. His neighbors complained to local officials, who came knocking at his door.

"Do you have a business in your home?"

"Yes."

"Do you employ nonfamily members in your business?"

"Yes."

"That is against city regulations. You have 30 days to rectify the situation."

Rectifying that situation meant restructuring his business. He had a strong enough desire to keep out of the nine-to-five environment that he found office space for the employees while he himself remained at home. (By the way, that situation cost him more than $1500 to correct!)

When I began, I lived in a typical suburb of a large metropolitan area. I called City Hall, asked for the planning and zoning department, and asked specifically about restrictions on home businesses in our community. Their answer may be typical of many areas. Home occupations are not licensed by my city. If I had an office site, I would then require a certificate of occupancy by the building inspection department. To stay within my zoning restrictions, I must have no outside signs, no employed persons other than the occupants of my home, no outside storage or machinery, no excessive traffic due to the business that might block the street, and, most importantly, no complaints. Again, I'm not saying these requirements are the same for your area, but they may be very similar.

If you inquire about obtaining the proper license and are told flatly that home businesses are prohibited, ask another clerk or go above his or her head. Inquire about a zoning variance or a legal way around the city law. The Entrepreneur Association tells a story about someone who applied for a license to conduct a research business from his home, but was abruptly told by a cranky city employee that all home businesses were illegal. He did some checking and was able to obtain a zoning variance enabling him to operate his business legally.[3] If this kind of prohibition happens to you, find out what kind of variance or conditional-use permit you can apply for and then make an effort to find someone in the bureaucracy who will help you with the additional paperwork required.

If you are operating outside of a city or town's jurisdiction, then contact your county government. Certain states also regulate various occupations and professions, requiring either a license or an occupational permit. Your state can tell you which occupations (such as real-estate brokers, insurance agents, plumbers, barbers, health-care professionals) require state approval. Other businesses require licensing by the Federal Trade Commission. They do not usually relate to home businesses, but contact the FTC if you feel your business may apply. Federally licensed businesses include radio and television stations, investment advisory services, etc.[4]

If you are a sole proprietor without employees, you may use your social security number as your business number on official forms. Or you can contact the IRS and obtain an application for an Employer Identification Number (EIN). You need this if you have employees or are set up as a partnership or corporation.

Tax Aspects of a Home Business

In recent years the IRS has closely scrutinized the self-employed, especially those who take the home-office deduction. One article reported that, at a national home business conference workshop, an IRS representative was quoted as saying that everyone who took a home-office deduction was red-flagged for an audit. Whether that's accurate or not, one of the best things you can do is get a good accountant, CPA, or tax professional to advise you, since tax laws change almost as quickly as Congress changes its mind. A tax expert will help you determine exactly which deductions you can take, and that is important since deductions reduce your taxable income and you pay taxes only on profits.

The Home-Office Deduction

The home business provides the taxpayer with an opportunity for a deduction generally not available otherwise: a deduction for the business use of your home. However, the workplace in your home must meet certain IRS criteria. For example, the part of your home utilized as a workplace must be used regularly and exclusively as one of the following:

1. Your principal place of business.

2. A place to meet or deal with your clients or customers in the normal course of your trade or business. (If this is the qualifying criterion you are using, the IRS requires that you must physically meet with clients or customers on your premises and that your meetings with them must be substantial and integral to the conduct of your business. Occasional meetings and telephone calls are not enough.)

3. If the part of your home used as a workplace is a separate structure and is not attached to your house or residence.

By regular use of your home-office, the IRS means that it is not just used incidentally or occasionally, but with frequency. Exclusive use means that the part of your home used for business must be used only for business, unless you use your home for providing day-care services or storing inventory, where the exclusive-use rule does not apply. If you are working at home for an employer and want to claim the home-office deduction, you must be able to substantiate that the use of your home is for the convenience of your employer. Be careful. Because of the exclusive use rule, a sofa bed, changing table, or family TV in your office could cause the IRS to disallow the home-office deduction.

Direct and Indirect Expenses

The deduction for the business use of your home involves two types of expenses—direct expenses and indirect expenses.

A *direct expense* is any directly identifiable expense made for the portion of the home used for business. Examples include:

• Painting the office

• Buying a new rug for it

• Replacing light bulbs

• Doing office repairs and maintenance

Indirect expenses are expenses incurred for your entire home that must then be allocated between your personal and business use. Examples of this type of expenses include:

• Utilities (Gas, electricity, telephone service)

• Property and liability insurance

• Real estate taxes

• Depreciation

• Rent (you don't have to own a house to get the deduction)

To determine the portion of the indirect expenses you can deduct, you must define the part of the home used for business as opposed to the rest of the home. Determine what percentage of your home is used for business by dividing the square footage of your office space by the total square footage of your home. For example, if you have a 1600-square-foot home and you have a 160-square-foot room set up for business, this would represent 10 percent of the home. You would then be able to deduct 10 percent of all of your indirect expenses.

The deduction for indirect expenses is limited. Please see your tax adviser for details. You can also request the IRS publication *The Business Use of Your Home.*

Regular Business Deductions

Other deductions available to home businesses are those generally defined as regular business deductions. These expenses are normally deductible by any business, not just those in the home, and they can include office supplies, phone bills, memberships in professional organizations, publications or books related to your business, equipment purchases, postage, and many other things. However, allowable expenses (or the percentages allowed) change, so consult with your tax professional. He or she can also sometimes alert you to upcoming changes in the law and make recommendations about the timing of certain purchases to give you the best tax advantage.

Keep good records so that you can take all the deductions available to you and so you will be able to substantiate your claims in case of an audit. Save all your receipts. If you incur a business expense and do not get a receipt, handwrite one.

When recording your business mileage, be sure to not only list the number of miles traveled and the date, but include your destination. When recording your entertainment expenses, include the amount and date of the expense, the place, the persons in attendance, and the relationship to you of those persons. Just saving restaurant stubs or credit-card receipts is not enough validation of your business entertainment expenses to please the IRS.

Estimated Tax Payments

If you are self-employed in your home, another tax consideration is to determine whether you need to make quarterly estimated tax payments. As a self-employed person, you have no employer to withhold taxes from your pay, so the burden falls on you.

Basically, you must make estimated tax payments if you meet the following qualifications. (If you fail to make these payments, you may be charged a penalty.)

1. If you expect to owe more than $1000 for the year (in excess of any withholding or tax credits).

And either one of the following:

2. If you don't expect your income tax withholding and credits to be at least 90 percent of your tax due for the year.

3. If you don't expect your income tax withholding and credits to equal your tax paid last year.

Estimated tax payments are due on the following dates: April 15 (for January through March), June 15 (for April through May), September 15 (for June through August), and January 15 (of the next year) (for September through December).

Sales Tax

Call your local tax agency to see if your product or service is taxable. The agency will give you the proper tax forms and a tax ID number. If you sell anything retail (and if you are offering certain services), you are responsible for collecting the appropriate tax (determined by where you live) and sending in quarterly payments.

One other note regarding your tax ID number: If you are buying items used in producing goods for resale, you don't have to pay sales tax on those items. Instead you present a copy of your resale certificate (issued by your taxing agency) when you make your purchase. Keep a copy of this certificate with you in your purse or briefcase at least until you set up accounts with your recurring vendors.

Finally, hiring an accountant or attorney is probably a lot cheaper than not hiring one. If you establish a relationship with a tax expert early in your business, he or she will be available to help you when the need arises. You should also establish a good relationship with your banker. These professionals can lend their expertise in areas unfamiliar to you, thus saving you money, aggravation, and legal problems.

6. *Determine your legal form.*

Decide whether you will operate your business as a sole proprietor, partnership, or corporation.

Sole Proprietorship

The sole proprietorship is the most common form of home-business ownership. *Starting and Managing a Small Business of Your Own*, by Wendell O. Metcalf, lists some pros and cons for sole proprietorship.

Some of the advantages:

1. Low start-up costs.

2. Greatest freedom from regulation.

3. Owner is in direct control.

4. Minimal working capital requirements.

5. Tax advantage to small owner.

6. All profits go to the owner.

Some disadvantages:

1. Unlimited liability (if the business goes under, you are personally liable).

2. Difficulty raising capital.

A sole proprietorship is the easiest and least costly way to begin. The only legal papers required are a business license and a fictitious-name filing with the county clerk. No separate tax returns are required, and you can combine your personal money with your company's money. However, in a sole proprietorship, business creditors can go after you personally. If your business goes bankrupt you must also declare personal bankruptcy or else pay off all the debts of the company from your personal funds. Your personal credit can be affected for years if your business goes bankrupt.

Partnership

A partnership is a legal form of operation in which two or more people basically operate together as sole proprietors. Each partner has equal authority in business contracts, unless spelled out differently by an attorney. Two advantages of a partnership are that it gives each partner freedom from the business at times and can provide an additional source of start-up capital. If you and your partner have brought equal and appropriate skills and abilities to the business, having a partner can provide assistance in making business decisions and free you to take time off for vacations.

However, one of the biggest problems with this type of operation is that *each partner is fully liable for the other partner's actions. Legal Aspects of Small Business,* by the American Entrepreneurs' Association, puts it like this: "In any legal or creditor action, each partner will be sued personally, with property, bank accounts, etc., being attached. If one partner skips town, the others are left holding the bag. Also, when an individual contributes assets to a partnership he retains no claim to those specific properties, but merely acquires an equity in all assets of the firm."[5]

Choosing the right partner is almost as difficult as choosing the right mate. He or she is with you for the long haul. You both have a lot invested in the relationship. You usually don't know nearly as much as you thought you did about the person when you entered the relationship, and often the worst in both people appears after you are "hitched." Even if you have known a person for a long time, don't leave anything to chance. Before you form a partnership, discuss with your prospective partner everything you can think of that might affect your business. Then have a lawyer assist you in drawing up legal papers. That way both of you are covered if your partner decides to leave the business, turns out to not work as hard as you, or changes his vision for the business. It is often difficult to remain friends with your partner if the business doesn't go as well as expected unless you have discussed all possible outcomes of your business at the onset of your partnership.

Corporation

A corporation is more complicated than other legal forms of business. It is a legal entity apart from you. It is responsible for financial obligations, not you personally, since you are technically an employee of a corporation—even if you own all or the majority of the stock. Here are some of the pros and cons of a corporation:

Advantages:

1. Limited liability. (If the business fails, your personal assets cannot be touched. The corporation protects your personal assets.)

2. Banks lend money more easily to corporations.

3. Profits can be delayed.

4. Capital can be loaned to you personally.

Disadvantages:

1. Possible double taxation.

2. Higher cost than the other forms of business.

Subchapter S Corporation

If you set your company up as a Subchapter S corporation, you take care of the double-taxation issue. "Subchapter S allows profits or losses to travel directly through the corporation to you and your other shareholders. If you earn other income during the first year and the corporation has a loss, you can deduct against the other income, possibly wiping out your tax liability completely. Subchapter S corporations are corporations that elect not to be taxed as corporations; instead, the shareholders of a Subchapter S corporation include in their individual gross incomes their proportionate shares of the corporate profits and losses."[6]

You do not always need the expense of a lawyer to set up your business as a Subchapter S corporation, although many business books will tell you otherwise. The forms are often easier to fill out than some credit applications, and you can easily file them yourself. The name you are using is checked by the Secretary of State's office (usually without an additional fee), and this office will tell you if someone is already using that name or a name closely linked to it. There are many online sources of incorporation resources.

7. *Choose your name and register it.*

The selection of a business name is an easy choice for some people and a hard one for others. Many simply lend their own name to their business. Others want a catchy, unique name. The most important thing in naming your company is choosing a name that describes what you do. Joan's Typesetting Service more clearly defines what Joan does than J.J. Inc. While J.J. Inc. may sound more professional, it doesn't tell you if Joan is an attorney, financial adviser, or hoozyhiemer manufacturer. Joan's Typesetting Service may sound boring, but it gets the point across. Remember to be descriptive in your name, not just unique.

If your business name is not your own, file a fictitious name certificate with the county. The fee is nominal (usually $10 to $100), and the county will inform you if someone else is already using the name you have chosen. The easiest way to determine the proper procedure for your area is to call your bank and ask what it requires for you to open up a business account. The bank people can then tell you where to go to take care of this requirement. If you incorporate, file your corporate name with your Secretary of State (who will also do a name search).

8. *Open a business account.*

Open a separate business bank account. It is vital that you do this in order to keep tabs of your business expenses and to ensure accurate record-keeping for business and tax purposes. If you were ever audited, it would be difficult to sort through things without a separate account. The cost is minimal, and all you need is either your fictitious name certificate, tax ID number, or business permit. Setting up the account is simple to do, costs very little, makes record-keeping and tax time simpler, and looks more professional than writing personal checks for business expenses.

9. *Have your printing done.*

One thing you will need is a logo. It may be as simple as your company name in a particular typestyle or more elaborate with graphics and artwork. Your logo is important because it is the common identifying element that ties all your printed materials together; therefore it should reflect the image or tone of your company. Your logo should also help clarify what your company does. If your business is targeted toward professionals or the financial industry, your logo should be straightforward, businesslike, and professional. If your business is crafts-oriented, let your creativity show in your logo design. What works for one type of business will be totally wrong for another.

Think of the image you want to create. Is your company serious? Lighthearted? Imaginative? Creative? Describe your image to yourself and then design (or have designed) a logo and choose a typestyle, paper stock, and color that reflect it.

Failure to match your business image with your printed output is a costly mistake to make. For example, a computer bookkeeping service probably would not want to have pink hearts on mauve paper for its business card, but that motif could be very appropriate for a children's party catering service.

Use your logo on your business cards, letterhead, and envelopes—and, if you choose, even more extensively. You can have it printed on your invoices and other forms or paperwork that your clients see. And of course if you do any advertising, your logo should be prominent. It is the unifying factor, the physical focal point, of the image you want your company to project. It establishes product or company identification among your clients or customers. It is also a professional touch. Many people will pass a first-impression judgment on your business based on the printed materials you give them. If you hand them a poorly done business card or send out a mailing with mix-and-match papers and plain number 10 envelopes that you can get in the grocery store, you are sending out a message that says, "I'm not serious enough about my business to invest in my printing," or "I don't pay much attention to detail," or "I'm really not very professional; I'm just a home business." Avoid all these signals. You do not have to be a graphics-arts major to create excellent-looking printing. Never put off having your printing done just to save money because in the long run you will lose money by approaching your business venture amateurishly.

Your local printer can help you with paper selections. If you find a particular paper that you like after looking at his samples, ask if there is anything comparable from another manufacturer that might be less expensive. You can often save money this way. Two paper companies may have a very similar type of paper, but one may cost more because it is harder to order or the supplier is out of state. Or the other paper may cost less because your printer bulk-ordered that paper last month and has an overrun sitting in the warehouse that he could let you have at a discount.

When you select your paper, consider the color, weight, and texture. In the right combination, these factors can enhance your company image. For example, if you deal in textiles (clothing, weaving), a heavily textured paper might be perfect. If you sell brass or glass products, you might want glossy stock. The paper you choose adds to your image. When you select the color of ink you will use, consider the color of your paper. You may like the color of ink you see in the sample book, but when it is printed on the color of paper you chose, you may get something a bit different from what you expected.

Now that you've decided on a logo and chosen your colors and your paper, you have several options: professional printing, laser or ink-jet printed stock, or a combination. If you're using a professional printer, select a printer that specializes in the type of printing you're doing. Don't go to the largest printing house in your town that does mostly four-color process jobs in large runs if you just need a simple printing of black ink on 20-pound bond. By the same token, you might not want a small "quick printer" if you have a complicated three-color logo with artwork and embossing. Do some telephone shopping and try to match your printing job with the right printer to get the best job possible at the best price. It may seem like all printers are the same, but they definitely are not. Another money-saving tip: If you can estimate the amount of letterhead and other materials that you think you will use in one year, your cost per piece for your printing will be much lower than if you were to have to reprint again later. However, this can backfire and cost you money if you move, or want to change or update your information, which is why many people opt for the next method.

Consider designing and printing your own stationery and business cards using readily available preprinted paper stock. With today's high quality laser and ink jet printers, you can produce very credible four-color brochures, business cards, and letterhead stationery at a fraction of the cost of printing house versions. Furthermore, you can print small quantities as you need them and update your material as prices, an address, or a telephone number changes or you add products and services. While cheaper, this option can often look less professional than traditional printing. I recommend the best quality you can afford.

Several companies sell designer paper, including papers intended for use as four-color brochures with blanks for you to add personalized print with your laser printer. This self-printing concept allows you to customize promotional material for each job, and the look is truly professional. Office Depot as well as catalog companies like Paper Direct and Viking carry some of these products.

Another option chosen by many people who want the professional look of custom printing but the price of laser printing is a combination of the two. Instead of using the stock companies, customize and have printed (with one color) one element of your stationery. Then run it through your laser printer. You can have your artwork scanned, and all your information (address, telephone number, etc.) can be easily changed.

Why so much emphasis on your printing? It is a major marketing tool. Shoddy work means poor representation. You need to put your best face forward.

Liz Curtis Higgs (profiled in chapter 2) is known for having a top-notch promotional kit and printed materials. She shares some "paper training" tips.

Lizzie's Rules for Paper...

1. There is no substitute for quality. Find the very best graphic artist(s), the best photographer, the best printer, the best paper, the snazziest stamps, the best mailing service. Determine where you want to be in this business in 3–5 years. Then design and spend accordingly.

2. Proofread everything three times yourself (hours/days apart). Then have at least two other perfectionists proof it. Work from a hard copy—it's tough to proof on the screen. Don't depend on your spell-checker to save you. Proofread backwards, too!

3. Start with small quantities. Don't be seduced by "another 5,000 only costs a few dollars more." Within a year, you'll want desperately to print something new, but will be burdened with all those full boxes. Save trees. Print small runs in the early years.

4. The only time I've ever regretted a business decision regarding paper materials is when I tried to save money or time. My motto now is *do it right the first time!*

5. If our businesses are for the Lord, then why do half-baked stuff? We honor the Lord when we do things well. Quality materials also bring in business.

Color

- Use a signature color and black
- Use bright, solid-color envelopes in various sizes
- Use basic, not trendy color(s)
- Let paper selection add a third color
- Don't use a 4-color press for a 2-color job

Cards and Letterhead

- My letterhead only lives on computer!
- Use specialty sheets, postcards, note cards

The Brochure

- 8.5 x 11 trifold or 11 x 17 one-fold
- Distinctive type style(s)
- Thematic touches
- Photos look best in black ink
- Include the basics:
    —Biographical info
    —Client quotes, endorsements
    —Photo(s), artwork
    —Client list, credentials
    —Name, address, zip, phone(s), fax, e-mail*

10. *Determine your record-keeping system.*

Keeping accurate records is vital to the success of your business. Don't leave anything to chance. The more detailed your book-keeping, the better. Routinely keeping track of your business on

---

* Used by permission, Copyright 1996, Liz Curtis Higgs, CSP, CPAE, P.O. Box 43577 Louisville, KY 40253-0577.

paper means that you will make more money because you will always know where you stand financially.

Hiring an accountant is an investment in your business. He or she can help you set up your books, alert you to all the tax benefits to which you are entitled, and keep you up-to-date in paying your taxes. (See chapter 10 for details on keeping records and setting up a system.)

11. *Establish a business plan.*

If you want to achieve your goals, begin by writing them down. For your home business, write your business plan. A good business plan will clarify your goals and give you a plan of action to achieve those goals. Include:

- A description of your business

- Your goals for future growth

- Start-up costs

- Finances: monthly expenses, monthly sales predictions, your income goal, sales predictions over a given period of time, a balance sheet (what you owe, what you have, and your investment in the company)

- Market research: your competition, your target market, your plan to reach that market (advertising and/or promotions)

- Production: how your work will be accomplished

- Management information: a bio of who's running the company

The SBA recommends the following information in your business plan if you are going to apply for a loan: the purpose of the loan, the amount of the loan, how you plan to pay it back, a description of the business, a financial profile of the owners and managers, a market description, and a list of available collateral.

A business plan is critical if you plan on getting a bank loan, but even if that is not your objective, take the time to write down your plan. You will know more clearly what your company is all about, how to explain that to other people, where you are headed, and how to get there.

One tax manager described it this way: "The first thing you need to do in starting a business is to sit down and develop your business profile in terms of who your customers are going to be, how you're going to market your services, and where your business is going to be in the next three years as you see it. Without those goals you really don't have anything to go after."[7]

12. *Get your initial equipment and supplies.*

After looking at your start-up priorities and the amount of money you have, then purchase, borrow, or otherwise obtain the necessary items you need to start your business. Be careful about what you buy. What you think you need in the beginning may not be necessary later on. Purchase your office equipment gradually as you discover, by working, just what your actual needs are. Don't rush out and buy office furniture, a computer, a telephone, a copier, and a fax machine before you are sure you need all that equipment.

Also, before sinking a ton of money into expensive equipment, check out all your options. Look at your list and then look around your house. Chances are that you can cross off quite a few items that way. In any case, a direct purchase of equipment may not always be the best bet. Comparison-shop carefully before you buy anything, especially the high-dollar items. Buying certain types of previously owned equipment or office items (such as furniture) can meet your needs and save you money. However, you should be extremely careful if you purchase used electronic equipment. It is best to buy this type of equipment new because then you get a warranty and a service agreement.

If you don't have the money you need to get started, leasing equipment might be an option if you foresee that you can generate some cash fairly early and then turn around and invest in your own equipment. However, if your start-up capital is that strained, you might do better to wait until you are in a stronger financial situation before beginning. Renting equipment can come in handy, however, if the equipment you own breaks down. I was once working on a big typesetting job when my computer crashed. I couldn't get it repaired in time to finish the job on time, so I found a company that rented the equipment and was able to meet my deadline. I still made a profit, even after paying the exorbitant daily rental rate. I didn't have to jeopardize my relationship with my client or risk losing the account by being unable to finish the job.

Again, if you are looking at office furniture, used (or "pre-owned," if you prefer) is often the way to go. Check out your home first. Do you have a spare desk in the garage or guest room that you can use? I confiscated my husband's desk until I had enough money in the business account to buy my own, and I also opted for one of our kitchen chairs since it was free. I bought inexpensive plastic shelving to hold my supplies (since they would be stored out of sight), and I borrowed the corner of another piece of furniture to hold my laser printer instead of buying the nice wooden printer stand that I really wanted. I may have wanted pretty new things to deck out my new home office, but I chose the most economical things instead. The smaller the cash outlay at the beginning, the better.

If you don't have much around your house that you can use, check your local paper, the "free" classified papers, consignment stores, and garage sales for quality office items such as furniture and filing cabinets.

When it comes to purchasing supplies, remember that you save money when you buy in bulk. (But try to accurately estimate how much of a certain item you can actually use, so that you're not stuck with 3,000 red pens just because they were half-price.) The best places to buy office supplies are generally the wholesale and warehouse stores.

13. *Decide where in your house you will locate your business.*

First it was the laundry room. Then it was the dining room. Then it was that corner in the bedroom. All these spots served as my home office at one time or another. But the ideal situation for a home office is a separate room specifically dedicated to your business. This separation keeps business physically (and hopefully mentally) from encroaching on the other areas of your life. One man I know had his new home built with 1000 square feet, complete with a separate entrance and atrium, reserved for his home business. Other people convert their garages or basements into offices. And some people have large spare rooms that would be perfect for their offices. The vast majority of people with home offices make do with what they have. Even if all you have is a small corner of a room, make sure this corner is devoted strictly to your business.

When you are deciding where to put your home office, keep in mind what your special needs are.

- Do you have the type of business that demands absolute quiet and concentration? Make sure your office has a door that can be shut.

- Does your office have a telephone jack?

- Are there enough electrical outlets, and are they in the places you need them?

- Will there be adequate space for all your equipment and supplies? Remember, space needs always grow as business does, so make sure you leave some room for physical growth.

- Will the space you have chosen work if clients must visit your work area? If you deal with businessmen in your service business and they have to meet with you in your work area, your bedroom would not be a good idea. But if they only need to drop off and pick up items, never seeing your workspace, a corner of your bedroom would be fine.

When outfitting your office, consider ergonomics—functional and comfortable equipment and work spaces. "As computer use accelerated, workers spending long hours at terminals began to show signs of physical strain that had never before been associated with desk work. Complaints of backaches, headaches, neck and shoulder tension, eye strain, and general irritability led to the emergence of the ergonomics design field."[8]

Such experts recommend the following:

• Writing and paperwork: Work surface should be 28½ inches from the floor.

• Typing or computer work: Work surface should be 24–27 inches from the floor.

• Computer monitor and copyholder should be 16–28 inches from the face.

During your start-up phase, determine what your ideal working environment would be like, the special needs you may have working at home, and what space you have available; then go from there.

14. *Get organized.*

Before you actually hang out your shingle, make sure your home is in order. Get rid of the clutter, clean out the closets or other areas of your home that need your attention, and know where all of your important papers are. In a nutshell, get your act together if you haven't done so before. Organize your home so that you can find things when you need them without having to tear the house apart in a mad search. Some may say this is no time to do your spring cleaning or household organizing, but I disagree. When you embark on something with as much potential stress as starting a home business, it helps to have the other areas of your life as neat and orderly as possible. If you have just spent the day doing start-up stuff, you don't want to find out at three o'clock that you have five minutes to locate and organize all the insurance papers that are scattered in three rooms of your house for the meeting your husband scheduled with a new agent.

Get organized about your daily schedule as well. Buy an organizer or appointment book and write down your appointments, phone calls, and "to-do" list. (I live by mine.) Leaving things to memory can leave you frazzled. Being organized in your home and in business affairs will make you feel better about yourself and will lead to a more peaceful and productive business and home life.

Starting up your business does not have to be a complicated, drawn-out, scary thing. Seek as many resources as you can for help and advice. Look at some of the options available in the Resources section of this book. A *Wall Street Journal* article on the start-up strain for a new entrepreneur reported that tapping outsiders for advice can reduce start-up panic, often at no cost: "If you can network and identify business owners who are established or retired, you can create a group you can go to for advice. Organized programs arrange for retired executives to provide small businesses with volunteer consulting help. Even before starting the enterprise the entrepreneur can talk to others who have gone through the start-up experience."[9]

Visit your library, talk with friends who have done it, and get all the advice and assistance you can. Seek counsel from both God and other people. The Bible encourages getting wise counsel: "Where there is no guidance the people fall, but in abundance of counselors there is victory" (Proverbs 11:14) and "Through presumption comes nothing but strife, but with those who receive counsel is wisdom" (Proverbs 13:10).

Above all, continue to ask the Lord to lead you as you lay the groundwork for a business that can glorify Him and bless you. "This also comes from the Lord of hosts, who has made His counsel wonderful and His wisdom great" (Isaiah 28:29).

6

Marketing: The One Thing You Can't Do Without

Janna knew the statistics all too well. A high rate of small businesses close in their first five years. And she was ending up in the wrong category.

Janna (not her real name) began her personalized service business with high hopes of succeeding and a heart for helping others. But she made the mistake that so many new business owners do. She didn't give much thought to her marketing plan. When she realized her mistake, she sought the advice of only one advisor—and then followed it. She spent her last $2,000 on a large ad in a national magazine. Unfortunately, it was not the magazine the people most likely to need her service read. She lost her business.

What is marketing anyway? Some may say, "Oh, that's advertising—and I don't have a budget for that. Besides, my business is too small to do marketing." But those folks would be wrong. None of us can afford not to market!

Christian Humility vs. Tooting Your Own Horn

Before getting into the nuts and bolts of marketing, let me try to dispel a concern you might have. For some Christians, deciding where the line is between being humble and being prideful poses a marketing problem. They read the Scripture "Let another praise you, and not your own mouth" (Proverbs 27:2) and they think they have no business promoting themselves. Genuine humility is indeed a virtue, but there is a real difference between praising yourself and promoting your business—and most of us need to promote our company in order to stay in business.

Writing your own résumé or press kit can be hard for us as Christians. We're tempted to say something like, "All these great things about me are true, *and* I'm one of the most humble people you'll ever meet." Even though everything in a publicity piece is true, writing it yourself (and promoting your business yourself) can seem too much like bragging. But remember, if you don't learn how to toot your own horn in the sense of letting others know about your business, the competition will speed by you.

If you are among those who find it difficult to promote yourself, you might try getting someone else to write your publicity material. If you write it yourself, focus on factual statements describing your product or service. One of the best ways to paint your business in the best light is to truly "let another praise you." Quote other people saying glowing things about you. Gather testimonials from satisfied clients or customers and ask their permission to quote them in your PR materials.

Needless to say, never overstate things to the point that they fringe on exaggeration or untruth. Don't try to be something you're not, for God honors integrity. Yet don't be shy about getting the word out about your business. Remember, if you don't, no one else will.

Marketing—What Is It?

Marketing is more than something into which large businesses sink a lot of money. It's more than advertising—but that's part of it. It's more than publicity—but that's included. It's more than direct sales—yet that's an essential element. Simply put, marketing is finding customers (or helping them find you) on an ongoing basis. The success of your business depends on your ability to sell your product or service again and again and again. After all, the single essential ingredient of a successful business is continuing customers!

You may have heard of the four P's of marketing: product (or service), price, promotion, and place. Since the place is our home and product and pricing vary by industry, we'll focus primarily on the promotional aspect of marketing. Marketing your home business can be quite palatable; it doesn't have to be as thick as "p" soup. Many marketing textbooks are dry and complicated, difficult for the home-based worker to apply to her often one-person band. To keep it simple, think of marketing as your plan to identify who your customers are, where they are, how you're going to reach them, and—most important—what they think about your business.

Peter Drucker, a leading business consultant, teaches that marketing is a person's entire business *as the customer sees it*. In *Do-It-Yourself Marketing*, author David Ramacitti's personal experience illustrates this principle. He describes going into a number of computer stores when he was ready to buy a computer. At one store the clerks were too busy talking to notice him. At another, no one could answer his computer questions. At a third store, the salesperson pointed to all the models available with a "Here's our line of products. Help yourself!" mentality. From all three stores he left empty-handed. He also describes a local restaurant that has wonderful "izza." While the food is good, the pot-holed parking lot is not, the restaurant's exterior needs painting, and obviously the neon sign is missing the P. He doesn't eat there much even though it has great food. In contrast, he also describes a local grocery store. It's a smaller store with the kind of staff that stops what they're doing to walk you across the store and show you to what you need. That store is where he buys most of his food. And where did he buy his computer? At the establishment where a salesman handed him a cup of coffee and then took notes as he described his computer needs. "All of these folks are 'marketing'—and probably don't even realize it," Ramacitti writes. "I'm perfectly willing to admit that my attitudes may be both unreasonable and unfair. But I would also strongly suggest to you that lots and lots of consumers make decisions about what they buy and where they buy it based on equally unreasonable and unfair attitudes."[1]

Everything about your business—but especially your name and printed materials—affects your marketing. Your carefully chosen, descriptive business name and all of your printed materials are marketing tools. Use them wisely to present a professional image. They say things about your business before you do.

Ramacitti's experience illustrates another key phrase in marketing: perception is reality. While that statement invites a philosophical debate, it's certainly a truth in the business world. If customers *perceive* your business in any negative way, the *reality* is that they probably won't buy from you. We may have a policy focusing on customer service, but if orders are three weeks late in arriving, our customers do not perceive us as being committed to quality customer service. Your policy may be real to you, but what the customer perceives is more important. That is why I like Drucker's take on marketing: We need to look at our business from the customer's viewpoint. This kind of focus on the customer can in fact be a godly response to the many passages in Scripture calling us to put the needs of others first and commanding us to serve. Companies—like Christians—do well to master the art of serving. That is one exciting aspect of home business marketing for Christians—we have an opportunity to serve others. It's no surprise that many home businesses run by Christians are also ministry oriented, focused on meeting other people's needs.

So, our marketing efforts need to focus on one thing—our customers. We need to consider who they are and how we're going to tell them about our product or service. We also need to focus our business efforts (from conception to sales) on our customers' viewpoint and how we can best meet their needs. So where do we start? Before we spend a penny on marketing efforts, we need to answer some questions about our market and our business.

Who are my customers? Write down everything you know about your target market.

- Who wants what I have to offer?
- Is my target market focused enough for success, yet broad enough to sustain my business?
- What are my customers like? What are the demographics of my audience (age, income, gender, occupation)?
- What are their shopping and buying habits?
- Is my product/service priced right *for them?*
- Who are my customers?

Your customer mailing list is one of the most valuable assets—if not *the* most valuable asset—in your business. Keep an updated list of the names, addresses, and, in some cases, phone numbers of your customers. Ask yourself what helpful information you should know about your customers in order to better serve them. To get this varied information try these ideas:

- Have new customers fill out an information card.
- Photocopy checks you receive. You'll have records of income as well as names and addresses.
- If you actually see your customers, invite them to sign your guest book or register to be on your mailing list.
- Get demographic information about your area at the library or from media representatives who provide this information to potential advertisers (along with their rate information).

Once you've established a mailing list, maintain it, add to it, and use it to send highly targeted direct mail to your customers. That mail can vary from information about new products or services you're offering, to notice of special sales or seasonal promotions you might have, to a newsletter providing usable information for your customers. And don't forget that important personal piece—the thank-you note.

You can also find out more about what your customers' needs are and what they think of your business by doing a phone survey. Call a few people on your list and ask them, "How am I doing? How can I better serve you?" Telemarketing calls surely aren't welcome, but a service call will probably be received with pleasant surprise. You can also find out more about your customers by asking them to fill out a *short* survey on a customer response card or interactively online.

Where are my customers? You not only need to know who your customers are, but where they are as well.

- Where are my customers going to buy what I'm offering?

- If my sales are retail (one-on-one to the consumer), what will replace the traditional "storefront"?

- Will customers come to my home to drop off work or buy my product?

- Will I go to them to deliver product or provide a service? If so, what distance am I willing to drive and how often?

- If I decide to sell wholesale, where are these buyers?

Having answered these questions, write down your specific markets. Begin by identifying where one particular market is for you, but as your business develops, be on the lookout for additional markets that will help you expand. Ask God for wisdom to help you think of untapped markets.

How will I reach my customers? This question addresses the issue that we primarily think of when we consider marketing.

- How am I going to let potential customers know about me?

- What vehicles will I use to sell what I'm offering?

- Will my sales be retail, direct mail, or wholesale?

What will I tell my customers? Answering the following questions will help you determine that.

- What need in my customer's life is my product/service meeting?

- What is unique about what I'm offering? How is it different from the competition?

- Can I succinctly describe my business and answer the preceding questions in a couple of sentences?

You must be able to articulately sum up what you have to sell. You also want to think about what you want other people to say about your business. Effective word-of-mouth advertising and networking depend on people being able to understand what you do.

So, right now, write down what need you are meeting and how you want to be known. Describe what you do in a couple of sentences *without jargon*. Speak in your customers' language. Besides rounding out your business plan, this brief summary statement will give you an immediate, articulate response to inquiries into what your business is all about. Nothing sounds more unprofessional than, "Oh, well, I make these…uhm…these things that are so cute. They're sort of hard to describe. They're for…" By now you've lost their interest. Or consider this response: "My company strategizes for the technological cross-lateral needs of APXIs." English, please. Being prepared with a pithy answer is not only helpful when you're explaining your business, but you will also be better prepared to write advertising copy or a brochure.

When will I tell my customers? This timetable is your marketing "attack plan." Without this schedule, producing the product or providing the service will take precedence over marketing. When deadlines loom or orders must be filled, we tend to focus on those. It's easy to get tunnel vision and forget to continue to market. A marketing schedule helps us continue to bring in business so that it's not feast or famine—and I know about that rhythm from my own desktop publishing business! At times I had my plate too full of deadlines and more work than I could handle, so I subcontracted some of the work out in order to meet the pressing deadlines. In those crunch periods, I focused all my time and energy on finishing the job for my present clients to the exclusion of marketing efforts. I was too busy to market! I had to finish the job and deliver the product! Then, once the deadlines were met, there I sat with not enough work to keep me busy. I learned from those times that a preplanned marketing schedule helps keep new business flowing in.

Once you've identified your customers and determined how and when you'll reach them, you need to decide how much time and money you should invest in marketing. To keep a steady stream of business, some experts say we should invest around 40 percent of both when we are looking for customers, and 20 percent when we are busy.

Networking and Word of Mouth

Two of the most successful ways to increase your business don't cost a cent. First, talk about yourself and, second, get others talking about you (your business, that is). When you talk about your business to your friends, family, colleagues, and associates, you are networking. The goal of networking is to develop relationships with people who might become customers or who can connect you with potential clients. When others talk about your business because they are satisfied customers, that's word-of-mouth advertising. You talk, and then they talk. This powerful, winning combination of networking and word of mouth is the key to a home-business person's success. So start networking. Then, as you gain business, those pleased customers will talk about you, and word-of-mouth advertising is born.

Networking

Begin networking by telling all your present connections about your new venture: friends, family, previous business associates, club or association contacts, and anyone else with whom you are in contact. Then look for local networking groups that you might join. Ask friends or associates to recommend networking groups. See the Resources at the back of this book for information on trade associations. Become active in groups whose membership could give you business or point you to business. Then work at establishing relationships rather than attending meetings once and trying to give your card to everyone there. Instead of looking for a general networking group, try to find one that has members in your target market. Also, you should already have some contacts if your business is something that you love (which I highly recommend). If you've turned a hobby or passion into a business, you no doubt already have numerous contacts.

It also helps to look for mentors in your field—an authority or success in your field who takes a special interest in you. Their guidance, business tips, and support can be invaluable. We all need cheerleaders and someone to whom we can go for advice. Another word you may hear or read about in reference to networking is "gatekeeper." Gatekeepers are business contacts who have access to possible clients, customers, or resources. Run through your current network to find the leads you're looking for. They can often put you in touch with others, who also know others (and so on) to lead you to the source, person, or information you need.

Finally, as many mothers who run home-based businesses know, one of the best ways to network is informally by integrating our business with our personal life. Simply put, we can talk about our business at our children's functions, church, and committee meetings. This kind of networking is particularly important since home-based workers are in an isolated work environment. Look for ways to discuss your business with as many people as possible in as many different environments as you can. Be assertive without being pushy or "pitchy." The book *Mompreneurs* puts it this way: "Networking... doesn't have to mean power lunches or racing to hand out business cards faster than the next guy at a big corporate function or trade show. Sure, this can be a good way to make prestigious contacts and land more clients and customers, but it's not the only way, especially for mompreneurs who have limited time and child care."[2]

In summary, consider these networking sources:

- Networking organizations
- Professional or trade associations
- Community involvement
- Mentors and gatekeepers
- Informal socializing

Publicity

Business generated by word of mouth is free marketing, but we must wait for it to happen. Publicity, however, can be free marketing we generate ourselves. And it is often one of a home-based business-person's best tools. Publicity can be a number of things—apart from paid advertising—that highlights you as an authority or resource in your field or in some way focuses the spotlight on you or your business. One of the nicest things about this kind of publicity is that others are complimenting you rather than you yourself. When people see a paid advertisement, they know the business itself was responsible for generating what was said. But when they read a feature article about you, or see a news story about your business on TV, or hear you on the radio, they see you in a different light.

It's one thing to read an ad touting "The Best Pies in Buford," but when the *Daily Buford Bugle* runs a review mentioning that you have the best pies in town, that's worth a lot more to consumers. That review will also add to your word-of-mouth referrals. You can then capitalize on that publicity by copying the review and sending it out with a coupon in a direct mail campaign, slipping it inside the brochures or newsletter you send to present and potential customers, or excerpting what was said about you and printing it on a postcard as a direct mail piece or response card. The fact that *you did not pay for what was said* about you is quite valuable. As Scripture says, "Let another praise you, and not your own mouth; a stranger, and not your own lips" (Proverbs 27:2). Publicity adds to your name recognition in your area or field, it generates goodwill for your business, and it adds to your credibility. Having a review of your product or service written about you is just one example. Let's look at some other forms of publicity.

Articles

Writing an article is one of the quickest ways to position yourself as an authority in your field. Even if you don't feel very authoritative, you—as a business owner—are an authority in your chosen field. You are undoubtedly in a business that you know a great deal about. So pass that knowledge on to others by offering helpful information to the readers. Why not write an article for your local paper, a magazine catering to your target market, or an industry magazine or trade journal in your field? The goal here is not to profit financially from the writing, but to generate publicity by positioning yourself as an authority in your field. If your business is computer training or service, you could write an article for your local or metropolitan newspaper on "Evaluating Your Computer Needs: Buying Enough Without Shooting Your Wad" or "Using Your Computer in Ways You Might Not Have Considered." If you provide personal or business organizing services, write an informative how-to piece called "Ten Ways to Beat the Paper Pile-Up Trap." Then rewrite the information with a new slant and submit your article to a trade periodical.

"But who would publish what I wrote?" You might be surprised. Publications of all kinds have space to fill. Small community newspapers are a great place to start, especially if you offer to write for free or in exchange for advertising space. Remember that you're getting your name out there as an expert and producing a clip file (featuring you as an authority) that you can copy and use in your other marketing efforts. Try these tips:

- Be professional. Ask the publication for writer's guidelines, enclosing an SASE [self-addressed stamped envelope], and then follow those guidelines when you write.

- Query first. Write a letter to the editor proposing your article and explaining why you're qualified to write it.

- When you pitch your article idea to the editor, describe how it would benefit his (or her) readers and be an asset to his publication. Be aware of what has been published recently, so you don't pitch the same topic covered just three months ago.

- Barter help from a writer. Triple proofread your article to make sure it's error-free when you submit it.

- Write the article *about* your business or yourself just as you'd like it to appear in the paper and include it in your media kit. You might be surprised to see that some papers will print your piece word for word (or close to it) if you write it in third person ("Lindsey O'Connor believes..." not "I believe..."), include the 5 Ws and H (who, what, where, when, why, and how), and write in inverted pyramid form (give the most important information first).

Radio & TV

Radio and television producers have needs similar to print editors. They, too, have space to fill—air space. If you are an authority in your field or have an interesting story, if you or your business is in some way newsworthy, or if you have timely information that would benefit the audience, then you may be just the person for a radio or television interview, profile, or story. News organizations look for authorities to interview about related stories they do. Last night my local news broadcast even interviewed a fiction writer specializing in murder mysteries for her input on a local murder case. If you have expertise in a certain area and feel confident talking to the media, let them know about you. You could also be the subject of an interview about your area of expertise. Authors are interviewed all the time by radio and television stations because, due to the mere existence of their books, the media know they have something to say about their topic.

But authors aren't the only ones getting in on publicity. Do you run a landscaping service? You could be the guest on a locally produced gardening program, or interviewed for a segment of a home-improvement show. Is there something unique about you, your experience, or the way you run your business? Do you have specific information that would be helpful and timely for the intended audience? Let the producers know about you.

- Send a well-written press release to a specific producer by name; never send to "Producer." Call to find out the current producer and spell that person's name correctly on the envelope.

- Target a specific program and detail how the producers might better serve their audience by including you on their show. Send a biography page (who you are and why you're qualified) and a list of questions they could ask when they interview you, so the producers' work is easier.

- If you've never given a radio or television interview before, write down the key points you want to convey on index cards and become thoroughly familiar with your topic. Practice! Have family or friends "preinterview" you. Listen to yourself on tape.

Press Releases

Publicity depends on having a well-written, professional press release. A press release (or news release) is usually one page long, double spaced, and sent—along with a cover letter—to producers, editors, and others in the decision-making, publicity-giving role.

Written with a news article tone, a press release describes an event, new product or business, or some aspect of your business that is newsworthy and timely. Local newspapers are often receptive to such releases and publish information in their business section or, if your release is announcing an event, community calendar section. Local papers will almost always cover the opening of a new business, so send a release when you begin your business.

Many small business owners say, "What could I possibly say in a press release to get publicity?" The majority of releases announce an event or activity: grand openings, new products, open houses, new services, and so forth. Other releases are feature oriented, keying in on people or the drama of a situation. And other releases immediately follow an event and report what happened or give results.

There's no reason why your business cannot generate several press releases a year. One source I found says small businesses should have no trouble producing six releases a year. Just study the business section of your local paper to see what businesses and events are being covered and why. Depending on their product, many times businesses are also featured in sections like Lifestyle or Health. Magazines often run feature articles or profiles generated by a press release.

While it's true that many press releases end up in the trash, editors and producers do need material. They have space or air time to fill and if you hit them on a slow news day or with an item that is of particular interest from a local angle, at just the right time and geared for their audience, you are helping to meet their need. Here are some reasons for sending out a press release:

- Your grand opening.
- Your 5th or 10th year in business.
- Your 1,000th customer.
- A workshop, seminar, or special event you're hosting.
- A speaking engagement you have with a local group on something related to your business.

- Your unusual way of promoting your product or service.

- Your business's unique solution to a particular problem.

- Something about your background (or that of a supplier, coworker, or customer) that is unusual or of particular local interest.

- A seasonal solution to a problem (like "when to prepare your garden soil for our area").

- A local tie-in to a national event ("Cucumber Awareness Week in Buford"). See *Chase's Calendar of Annual Events* at your library.

Also, while you're at the library, look for some books that give examples of well-written releases that will get coverage. Then go one step further and produce a media kit. Add a cover letter to your release and put them in a nice folder along with black-and-white glossy photos of yourself or your product, a sample if applicable, and a copy of anything that's been written about you or your business. A media kit is an invaluable marketing tool for gaining publicity.

One more point. I've been on both ends of a press release. I've written them for my business, but I've also received them in my broadcast work. The ones that sounded like an advertisement hit the trash can during the first paragraph. Avoid that at all costs.

Press Release Dos and Don'ts:

Do make it:

Timely

Concise

Ready to print as is

Specific and easily understood

Journalistic in style (the 5 Ws and H)

Unique and interesting

Factual, not opinionated

Newsworthy, of local interest, or interesting feature material

Don't write:

A sales pitch or self praise

To the consumer (do write in third person)

More than one message or theme per release

Seminars

Do you enjoy public speaking? Do you like to teach something you know about to others who want to know more? Presenting a seminar or workshop on a topic in which you are well versed is a great way to increase your name recognition, establish you as an authority, and generate future business. (One woman I know has a full-time business giving seminars around the country, and she started by presenting her material to small groups in her living room!) Leading seminars and workshops works particularly well for service and information businesses. Teaching a class at a local community college or community center can also increase your credibility and help you network.

In some instances you can even offer products for sale at the seminar site in what's called "back-of-the-room sales." Books, audio- and videotapes, CDs, and products related specifically to your topic often do very well. You might offer discounts on orders placed at the time of the seminar or a special incentive for buyers if they mention they attended your seminar. Even if you can't sell directly at your speaking event, you will obtain good leads for future business. You can also generate additional publicity by having your event included in local newspaper or radio "community calendars" that advertise such events as a service to their audience.

I attended a workshop on "The Internet Marketplace." There were no product sales that night, but the speakers let us know about the local Internet service provider sponsoring the event and making themselves available to open the doors of cyberspace for us. The workshop provided a twofold service to the community: it was a free chance to learn about Net business, and sponsors offered to get people set up to surf the Web that evening (with a discount for attendees). In fact, that event made them the first company I thought about calling several weeks later when I was ready to enter cyberspace.

Not only have I attended workshops, but I've also done all-day seminars with paid registrations, workshop presentations, and shorter talks for numerous groups. I've found that it's not only great for business because of increased credibility, publicity, and sales, but it's also a wonderful way to get in touch with your audience or market. There's nothing like face-to-face contact with the people you're trying to reach. It really helps you keep in touch with your market and enables you to see those you're trying to serve as real people, not just sales numbers. I've especially been blessed by the ministry aspect of such events. It's wonderful to get to talk individually with people and even pray with them about their needs.

Money for Your Marketing

Before looking at direct marketing (direct mail and promotions), advertising options, and service, let me first offer a word of warning about spending money in your home-business marketing campaign:

Be cautious. Don't automatically decide to spend your marketing dollars on A & B just because your competition does. Have a budget, a plan, and specific goals you want to accomplish with a targeted market.

Do your homework. Before you spend a penny, read and talk…a lot. Volumes of books have been written on every aspect of marketing. These detail the methods as well as the pros and cons of each option available to you. Also be sure to talk with people who are succeeding with the marketing method you're considering. Learn what frequency (how often) and duration (how long) experts recommend for the approach you want to take. In other words, don't just place a single ad or send out a postcard once. Know what pulls results.

Have a plan. Don't use the hit-and-miss approach: "I'll try a newspaper ad this month." Have an overall picture of what marketing methods you're going to try in a given year. Think in terms of your overall campaign, instead of "What can I try now to get customers?"

Have a budget. Calculate the cost and compare it to the results. In the words of "guerrilla marketing" expert Jay Levinson, "Anyone who engages in direct marketing without knowing with certainty the exact cost to acquire a new customer, the lifetime worth of that customer, and the profit per sale, is only playing with marketing, not taking it seriously. Marketing is too expensive to be treated capriciously."[3]

So just how much should you spend on direct mail or advertising aimed at getting new customers? Here's an interesting guideline: "If you can reasonably expect to recover the cost of getting that new customer in two years, give or take a few months, then it's probably worth doing."[4]

Direct mail

"But I don't want to spend money to produce someone else's junk mail," you may think. You may have a point, but consider some creative and effective ways that you can use certain kinds of direct mail to solicit orders, generate requests for information, or remind your customers that you're available. Direct mail includes postcards, sales letters, brochures, newsletters, fliers, catalogs, coupons, and customer thank-you notes. There are basically two reasons to send direct mailings: to generate new business and to touch base with existing customers. But before you have 2000 letters printed and mailed to "occupant," beware of the biggest mistake inexperienced direct mailers make: Their mailing list is not targeted enough. Shotgun-approach mass mailings are expensive and have an extremely low return. If you're too broad in your focus, your efforts automatically become junk mail, and that's a waste of time and money.

A highly targeted mailing list is key to direct-mail success, and you can tighten your list using information from your network of contacts, list brokers, and directories from organizations that you or your prospects belong to, or by trading lists with businesses that have the same customer profile as your business, particularly if your businesses complement one another.

Your House List. By far, the most valuable asset your business has is your house list, the names and addresses of your customers. *Always* get the names and addresses of your customers. Frequently update your list and don't take it for granted—use it regularly to increase customer awareness of your business; generate goodwill; inform them of sales, new products, or services; and let them know about changes in your business. To increase response and enhance your relationship with your existing customers, personalize your mailings to them. Instead of mass printing thousands of direct mail pieces, do small runs on your laser printer. Also use mail merge and list software to make your mailing as personal as possible. If your product or service is in a higher-priced category, follow up this type of mailing with a phone call.

Direct Mail Tips

- Narrow, narrow, narrow the list.

- Send useful information (not junk mail).

- Make it personal.

- Repeat your mailing several times to prospective customers.

- Code your address so you can see which marketing tool is pulling what response. (Add a department name or number or an extension to your box number: "P.O. Box 735B" or "Dept. H."

- Be specific about why you are contacting them. Repeat the message in the piece.

- Include a response device—something that will make them take action (scratch offs, stickers, timed discounts, "mention this ad and receive…" offers, rebates for referrals, etc.).

Promotions

One of marketing's proverbial 4 or 5 P's, *promotions* offers a varied way to produce immediate sales, often face-to-face with your customer. Here is just a smattering of suggestions:

Sampling. Give away a sample product or a one-time offer of your service. If people like it, they'll buy again. If you offer a service, try giving away some of your time to generate initial word-of-mouth advertising.

Contests and Giveaways. Sponsor a contest related to what you do. It will promote your business and help you add to your mailing list. Everyone loves something free. Give away something with what you sell. Offer a "baker's dozen," an additional quantity, a free product with every sale, or "buy 5/get one free." (Note: there can be legal restrictions on some contests.)

Price Incentives. Some say this is the oldest promotional method around, and it can be very effective. Hold seasonal sales or clearance sales, offer introductory discounts, and distribute coupons. Everyone loves to save money, so be creative and use various incentives to get people to make an immediate purchase from you.

Trade Show Exhibits. Most industries have trade shows every year, and many industries offer countless places for you to exhibit at all across the country. If your product or service is visually oriented or you would benefit by demonstrations, consider the trade show option. Carefully choose the type of show and consider attending one to gather information before you spend the money to exhibit. Reserving exhibit space and setting up your booth can be very expensive, so talk to home-business owners in similar businesses to see if exhibiting has been profitable for them. Don't exhibit with a shoddy booth. If you need help creating an attractive booth, think about hiring a consultant. You might also consider sharing booth space to cut down on costs or offering to speak at the show in exchange for booth space. I've done both of these things in the past and saved money.

Advertising

I made a marketing mistake early in my desktop publishing business. I thought, "Advertising! To bring in new clients, I need to advertise!" So I bought a display ad in my local community paper (not my larger metropolitan paper) offering my skills and services. I was shocked when I received only one response to that ad, and that didn't even result in a sale. My mistake? The paper's readership was the wrong audience. When I began to network with other people working in desktop publishing, with printers, and with small companies that produced newsletters and materials I specialized in, I found clients. My advertising dollars should have gone to a Yellow Pages listing, not a broad-market display ad. I hadn't thought through my target audience carefully enough.

Classified Ads

While display ads do work for many businesses (just look at how many ads there are), do your homework before you sink advertising dollars into such a broad-based medium. Both producing a display ad and purchasing space for it are costly. A home-based person might want to consider a classified ad instead. This type of space is cheaper to buy, and you don't have the cost of producing your ad. Plus, customers are often ready to buy. You can purchase classified space in shoppers (local and national), your local paper, trade journals, and consumer magazines. Remember that the first word in your ad is the most important.

Yellow Pages

This is a great way to advertise your home business particularly if your business is service oriented and geared for your local market. For the money, you get great visibility—which is important since you have no storefront. In the past, only businesses with a separate business line could advertise in the Yellow Pages, but now some areas offer "home office" options. Check with your local phone service provider to see what is available in your area. A listing in the Yellow Pages could be the number one item in your marketing plan if you serve local customers.

Trade Journals & Directories

Peruse a trade association directory at the library or an online source, and you'll see that there are associations and related publications and membership directories for every possible industry, trade, and profession. Some organizations give their members free listings in their directories with membership or if they advertise in their journal. Advertising in these publications allows you to market to a very narrow audience.

Broadcast

Radio and television advertising is not the medium for most home-based people just starting out. First, it's expensive and, second, it reaches very broad audiences. However, if your target market is to a wide range of consumers, if you can afford it, and if the demographics hit your target market, you might want to consider local television and radio. Rather than approaching the network affiliates, ask for demographic and rate information from local independent and cable TV stations. Some cable stations have public access channels that offer free or low-cost programming time to the community. Radio, the portable medium, also hits a very broad market, but it can be better targeted since different formats (country, Christian, public radio, and so on) have different demographics. As with all marketing efforts, be sure you know your customer well before you use the broadcast media.

Card Decks

These packets of postcard ads try to generate either orders or information requests. The cards are usually wrapped in cellophane and mailed to a targeted market. I've received card decks from home-school suppliers, those selling products to ministries, and businesses with accounting-related products. While card decks can be highly targeted and still reach a vast audience, an ad usually costs in the $1500 to $2000 range. But two women I know have written articles for magazines that distributed card decks in exchange for free or reduced-cost card deck ads.

Online

This marketing option gets its own chapter. Keep reading.

Advertising Specialties

This category includes all the coffee cups, pens, refrigerator magnets, and the like that advertise a company. (You might be surprised by how many such items you have in your home right now!) Numerous advertising specialty companies (check your phone book or online sources) have catalogs of thousands of products to personalize and thereby remind your customers about you. To some degree, these items also advertise to noncustomers. These products are great for initial promotions and can keep your business name in people's minds, especially if you choose a product that's related to what you do and that will be used or seen often.

Service

If you have a huge marketing budget and hire both a snazzy marketing consultant to advise you and an advertising agency to produce your campaign, but you forget one thing, your efforts and expenses will all be for naught. That one thing is this: Never forget to focus on meeting the needs of your customers or clients. In a word, never forget service. We're back to what was talked about at the beginning of this chapter. Look at every aspect of your business from the customer's perspective. Are you meeting her needs? How well are you serving him? When we are motivated to serve and have a genuine desire to help others, two things happen. First our customers will know it and our service will make an impression. Mediocre to bad service is far too common. That's why quality service fuels word-of-mouth advertising, a home-based business person's best tool.

But, serving your clients is important for more than making an impression or a sale. All that we do for others in our businesses should be motivated by our faith. As a Christian first and a Christian businessperson second, we can be beacons for Christ. As we serve, people will see that our actions are motivated by Christ's example. After all, He came not to be served but to serve (Matthew 20:28). Nothing can damage our witness more than professing to be Christians and then conducting business without integrity. This inconsistency not only damages our business (and personal) reputations, but it also damages the body of Christ. A heartfelt desire to serve and a high ideal of integrity in all we do should be our bywords for the sake of our businesses as well as for the sake of our witness for our God.

Now this chapter has presented a rather simplified approach to marketing, but then most of us home-basers have simplified businesses compared to Fortune 500 companies, so we don't need the IBM marketing model. However basic these ideas seem, use them as a springboard to further study and learn all you can about marketing. Don't let the fact that you are working alone from your home keep you from becoming an expert in how to market what you are selling. A dear friend of mine, Posy Lough, who has run a home business for many years, is a genius at marketing. She once read every book that was required reading for MBA students at a well-respected graduate school. No wonder she knows so much! You can too if you read, read, read!

Finally, a carefully researched and well thought-out marketing plan is important, but it's not the whole story. Oh, we need to know our customers well, we need to determine the best options for our particular business, and we need to learn what our marketing efforts will cost and the expected return. But even as you work on a marketing plan, be aware that sometimes God will bless you beyond and in spite of all of your efforts (or mistakes). Sometimes, for instance, you might "just happen" to sit next to someone on the plane who needs your services and becomes a client; you will be introduced to someone who gives your business publicity; or word of mouth takes off and networking opportunities open up. As a Christian I choose not to view these as coincidences, but as God's intervention in the details of my life and, yes, my business. Therefore, to the four P's of marketing I add one more: prayer. We must always remember to bathe our marketing plans in prayer, asking God to not only bless our businesses but to enable us to minister to others by serving them.

Top Ten Marketing Tips for Home-Based Businesses *

1. Successful marketing spotlights your company so that your product or services appeal to your targeted customers.

2. Market your company whenever the opportunity arises! Do not let the fear of rejection or of making a mistake hold you back from any opportunity.

3. Target those prospective clients who are very likely to buy from you. That's the quickest way to build your business with limited time and money.

4. Spotlight your product or service and explain how it can significantly improve your customer's business or life.

5. Be able to tell a prospective client in one minute why your product is wonderful and different from the competition. Be clear about the value you offer!

6. Remember that every element of your business—from business cards to packaging—helps create your market position.

7. Everything you say, do, or write should be in alignment with your market position. A consistent message will be recognized.

8. Marketing has one purpose—and that is to get sales!

9. When you market your work successfully, the money and fun will follow!

10. Marketing is the cornerstone of a successful business and should be a daily priority. Log your marketing activities and expenses for one month and evaluate your approach. Note successes!

* Source: Claire Cross & Associates interview

How to Narrow Your Market *

1. Determine the products/services that your clients value the most.

2. Identify the clients you want to do business with—and be aware that there are plenty of people with whom you do not want to do business.

3. Choose market segments that are easy for you to reach. Consider company size, number of employees, industry type, location, or the characteristics such as age, sex, or lifestyle of your ideal client.

4. Segmenting helps you narrow your market focus and get a possible 10 percent response with less time and fewer dollars expended. (For example, postcards mailed to all businesses in a zip code could get a 1 percent response, whereas mailing to a specific business type could get a 10 percent return.) Pursue the least costly route and the most likely to buy segment of your potential market.

5. Your most valuable market is the one to which you are currently selling. Increase your effort here in order to increase your market share.

6. Customer referrals are highly likely to become customers themselves. Let these referrals know you want to work with them.

7. Keep a list of 10 prospects posted all the time. Target your efforts until one becomes a client—and then add a new client to the list!

8. Use customer evaluations to help you focus your efforts.

9. Keep a close eye on your competitors.

* Source: Claire Cross & Associates interview

Home Business Online

With a computer and phone line, you can have connections around the world—instantly. The Internet is about information, and it does it well. You can access and then download everything from the words to the "Gilligan's Island" theme song to a picture of the Mona Lisa to a video of lava flowing over rocks at ECNZ Waihianoa aqueduct from the Ruapehu volcano. And all just a few key strokes away!

So exactly how can going online help your business? It offers:

- Instant, 24-hour access to information about your business and online sales via your website
- Measurable impact
- Instant feedback
- A wealth of resources and information
- Versatility
- Sources of income
- Relatively low cost
- Unlimited room for expansion
- Interactive capabilities with customers from your home

Please note that some of the information in this chapter will be outdated by the time the pages come off the presses. The online world is changing so rapidly that we'll talk more "how-to" than "where-to" or "what-to."

This chapter is divided into three parts. If you are already online and familiar with the Web, skip the first section ("Getting Online") and go to the next section ("Benefiting from the Internet") for ideas about how your business can benefit from an active role on the Web. If you enjoy other people's websites but haven't considered establishing your own, read the last section ("A Professional Site"). You might be surprised by how easy it is to have customers contact you at www.yourname.com! (By the way, this entire chapter was written by electronic means: the research, interviews, and even a survey, were all done online.)

Getting Online

Not too sure about the Internet? Neither was Jill Bond, a full-time mother and part-time author, speaker, and founder of three international ministries. Join this home-business woman as, throughout this chapter, she shares her journey from cyberspace reluctance to creative use of the Internet.

> **Jill:** *I hesitated to go online because I felt I had enough to do without adding one more access point. I was already receiving hundreds of letters each day; I didn't need more mail. But my online friends kept telling me of all the benefits....So I signed on to one of the main services. Immediately I was impressed that, instead of adding work to my already filled schedule, it reduced my workload. Since then, we see the blessings the Web can be. We've added a many page website (www.bondingplace.com), and we change pages each month. Instead of publishing a hard copy of our magazine, we only print it online now at $\frac{1}{100}$ the time and money and triple the yearly readership.*

I like the analogy of roads and vehicles that Mark and Wendy Dinsmore use in their book *Homeschool Guide to the Internet*. Just as roads link cities around the world, the Internet links computers. Just as cars, buses, and planes use these roads to transport drivers, the Worldwide Web transports individual users to libraries, shopping malls, and information sites. Just as personal cars transport you to church, a friend's house, and meetings, online services send you into your friend's home via e-mail and into meetings via forum chat rooms. Also, just as you use your car to take you to the mall, government office, or library, you can use your online service and the Worldwide Web to access this information. Just as there are many makes and models of cars, buses, and various transportation services, a variety of providers give you access to the Internet. For instance many search engines (bus services) exist to get you from point "A" (your computer) to point "B" (the Library of Congress), and they vary in performance, speed, and ease of use.

Test It First

If you are hesitant about going online, give it a test-drive. Many public libraries have Web-accessible systems available for the public, or perhaps you could log on at a friend's home. Several of the major providers offer free software and a free 30-day trial membership.

You'll notice right away that writing on the Internet is quick, to the point, and filled with acronyms,[1] symbols, and "net-ese" (online language: netiquette[2], emoticons[3] :), web-sters[4]). It won't take you long to pick up on the abbreviations, and you'll find most chatters quite friendly.

Equipment and Providers

Modems. Years ago a modem was considered a luxury or an "as the budget allows" peripheral, but today home computer systems come with a modem installed. Developers are constantly making breakthroughs in this technology, so you might want to consider upgrading to a faster modem as your online work increases.

Kay Hall, author of *The Ministry Macintosh* and columnist for several computer magazines, has a great suggestion for upgrading equipment called "The Next to Last Rule." She doesn't upgrade until the next level of technology comes out, and then she either waits for the natural price reduction on the previous grade or she looks for someone who upgrades right when a new product comes out and buys that person's old model. She doesn't have the latest model, but she gets a still-current model at reduced prices.

Providers. Shop around for the provider that best fits your needs. Before you publicize your e-mail address, be comfortable with your provider and plan to stay with them. As difficult as it is for customers to track you down if you change physical addresses (at least the post office forwards mail), it is not ideal to automatically forward e-mail or to inform others of an e-mail address change. When you're shopping around, look at these factors:

Fees—You can get an e-mail address for very little and, in some areas, for free (e.g., education nets for teachers, Yahoo). To find services that give you free Net access, you just have to wade through all the advertising.

As you shop, you'll find online providers offering a variety of services. Some offer unlimited Internet use for one low fee, while others give you a set number of hours for a fee and then charge you for additional time spent online.

User ID (your e-mail address)—It really does help to have a catchy or easy-to-remember e-mail address. Some services allow you to use your name, like janesmith@email.com or JanesCrafts@ provider.com. The simpler and more recognizable, the better. Some services even allow you multiple IDs for one fee, enabling you to organize your mail according to different aspects of your business or have a private personal account to handle nonbusiness e-mail.

Jill: *Since we have various ministries, we use different e-mail IDs to make it easier for clients to reach us and for us to identify their needs. We also have separate IDs for personal mail to individual members of our family. We have addresses tied into specific* *requests, monthly articles, surveys, and so forth. Since many people learn about us via television or radio interviews, having an easy-to-remember e-mail address or Web address is critical. It's like having a great 800 number that spells out your company name.*

Accessibility—The service may offer fantastic prices and custom user IDs, but if it doesn't have the equipment to maintain the volume of traffic, you may get a busy signal 90 percent of the time you try to log-on.

Extras—While some services merely offer e-mail capability, others are linked to the Web and have wonderful forums and chat rooms.

Local Access—Check for a local access phone number. You don't want to have to pay long-distance fees in addition to online fees. Some services offer an 800-number for access, but charge an additional hourly rate. Those fees can add up fast if you need to do much research.

New Breakthroughs in Technology—Even if you don't have a computer, you might look into systems on the market that give you complete Web access through small electronic devices or a television. As Internet technology advances, more and more breakthroughs will make our work easier.

Benefiting from the Net

If you're on the Web now, you might not be getting all your money's worth. The Web can be a powerful tool for every aspect of business from initial research and product development to marketing and client contacts.

Abundant Information

Accessing the Internet has helped business for freelance writer Peg Roen, who says information is what she wants—and she's learning how to find it.

First and foremost, being on the Internet has helped me meet deadlines. When you have a deadline, every minute counts. Now that I'm online, I can squeeze out three extra days by not having to send a disk and a hard copy through the mail, and not having to use overnight or priority mail saves me money. Before, I had to build three days into my schedule to allow mail time. Now I just e-mail the editor a message and send the document as an attachment.

Being on the Internet also cuts my phone bill down. I pitch a story or check on the progress of a story by e-mail instead of calling. It's also more considerate of the editor's time. E-mail is more to the point and more convenient for him or her.

As far as doing research online, I'm very hungry for information, but I just don't always know where to look. Often the searches will come up with 2000 entries or more of the thing I'm looking for. I've learned that, when I'm reading magazines and I'm interested in getting more information on a particular topic, I look for the Internet addresses. If there's an address, then I can get past the search and learn more quickly.

The Worldwide Web provides instant access to information sources that will save you time and, in many cases, money. From governmental publications to magazines online, you can search the Web to give you information for making decisions about your home business. Thousands of sites—including the Small Business Administration at www.sba.gov—offer helpful information to the entrepreneur. Since so many of these sites are linked to other sites, you could surf and search for hours by merely clicking highlighted addresses on various home pages. When you come up with 75,000 possible sites, you can be overwhelmed by this wealth of information. Yet with practice you'll learn how to use the search engines to your advantage and fine-tune your searches. Two basic kinds of search engines are "exhaustive" and "prescreened."

In addition to using search engines, you'll want to take advantage of the "water-cooler effect" of forums or e-mail discussion groups. These bring together people with common interests for online discussion. As you research your particular niche, check out as many discussion groups on your subject as possible. You can locate some of these through websites and via online services. For example, if you want to know how to set prices in your up-and-coming pet grooming service, you can gain a wealth of information from other groomers around the country via online discussions. Log on to an animal forum, search for the subtopic of groomers, and then ask all your questions. Since you aren't local competition, other groomers are usually very willing to help. They also want ideas from you. Many professionals swap ideas on forums specific to their industry.

As you line up suppliers, you'll find the Web most helpful at such sites as the Thomas Register (www.thomasregister.com) and several "Yellow Pages" sites (search). You can also subscribe to online magazines and newsletters about your topic and tap into the experts in your field.

Jill: *As a writer, I find I'm using the Internet for more than 75 percent of my research, including finding contacts, doing primary and secondary research, conducting personal interviews, and verifying information. I can even access my local library comfortably in my own home—drastically reducing my workload and time away from my beloved children. I use it not only for the actual articles and chapters, but also in developing my proposals and selling my works (substantiating market, viability). I also bounce ideas off my friends and test-drive some of my articles by them before I submit them to editors. There are some marvelous writers' forums and great websites. One of my favorites is the Christian Writers Fellowship (http://www.gocin.com/cwfi/ writer~1.htm).*

Respectable Impact

Some home-business people are discovering that having a presence on the Web is strengthening and helping their business in numerous ways including expanding their market, scope, and client base.

Hot Prospects: While some companies actually sell products via their sites, others use their sites to prescreen customers and generate a mailing list. In most cases someone interested in your topic or product has searched for you. That alone makes these Web contacts excellent prospects for mass mailings. Also, these contacts are usually prequalified in that they have documented their interest and have some disposable income.

International Markets: The opportunity to instantly reach—via the Web—people around the globe is unprecedented. E-mailing to Bangkok doesn't cost any more than e-mailing to Bangor, Maine.

Cross-links: As the Web expands, so does your market—not just in terms of potential clients, but also in the number of possible electronic bulletin boards, e-mail discussion groups, search engines, and other sites for links. Once you have a site, you'll want to search the Web for sites that have a similar topic, product, or service. Your Web designer might include this search or charge extra for it. Most of the links I've seen have a section for links to similar sites. Ask the manager of those websites to add your site (or e-mail address) to the list. Some managers will want information from you, some will check out your site, and some will want a few sentences about your business, while others will list anyone. With just a few days of work, you could have your company listed on hundreds of websites. Multiple listings help Web surfers find you as they leapfrog from one site to the next using cross-link functions without going back to the search engine. Finally, while the Net does offer some paid advertising (as in banner ads), most home businesses don't have the budget for that big an expense. But good links on appropriate sites work very well and are a sort of electronic word-of-mouth endorsement.

Some individuals, however, offer "links-for-a-price," charging fees for these links. Paying for links is like buying a paid endorsement.

(It's similar to a theater critic receiving kickbacks for a good review.) Links-for-a-price wouldn't seem unethical if they'd post warnings that these referrals are merely paid advertisements. Still, enough great people are on the Web, providing real service, that you shouldn't ever have to pay for a link.

Link Centers: Some companies serve as a kind of chamber-of-commerce center. They charge fees for their services because that is their business. Net users visiting their sites go in knowing they are looking at advertising. These sites do serve both the small entrepreneur and those who use it, but everyone realizes that they're looking at paid ads. Beware of any service that combines "reviews" and "referrals" with paid links.

> **Jill:** *I've been blessed to expand our ministries worldwide. For example, anyone worldwide can just key in the word "autism" and our PREACCH ministry (our service for families with autism) comes up on most of the search engines. Instantly they are in contact with hundreds of other like-minded families and added to our prayer list. There is no way I could touch that many lives through any other earthly media. What we've found is that people visit our site and like it and then go back to their other favorite sites and ask them to put a link on their site to ours—the effect is astounding.*

Instant Response and 24-Hour Access

Have you planned any mass mailings? You might have heard that a 0.3 to 5 percent response rate is good, and it might take months to see the full impact of your efforts. Yet, with a homepage or website, you get instant feedback. You can change policies, prices, or shipping instructions in moments. You can also survey your clients for their preferences and have the results tabulated within seconds. Also, your office hours don't matter on the Web. Anyone at anytime can access your website or send you e-mail. You can access your databases and answer your e-mail as your schedule allows. Furthermore, in most cases, your clients find you.

Gentle Promotion: Since direct advertising is taboo in many Web forums, you might wonder how you can use them to promote your company. Kay Hall has found a way to help others and gently promote her books, all within "netiquette" guidelines and without being sneaky. She spends a few minutes every day logging into forums or e-discussion groups that have some content related to her writing topics. She scans the messages and, when she knows an answer to someone's question, she replies with a post and signs her name—Kay Hall, author of *The Ministry Macintosh* (or whichever book is most applicable). The questioner then has the answer (which is what they were after) as well as Kay's e-mail address to contact her directly. Others reading these posts will learn from Kay's expertise and benefit also since posts in forums are open for others to read. Besides establishing Kay as an expert, this method has effectively opened doors and brought in referrals for her.

Mass Mailings: You can use the Internet for two different types of mass mailings—solicited and unsolicited.

Solicited: You can collect e-mail addresses just as you do for written mail—with permission. Periodically, you could write an article about your services and mail it to all your e-mail contacts. You write the article once and then address the letter to your mail group. The system does all the rest, and you can reach thousands within seconds. One more note. Always make it simple to remove someone who wants to be taken off your list and respond promptly to his or her request.

> **Jill:** *Many friends send me monthly or weekly e-magazines, and I enjoy them and find them very helpful. I also receive alerts from several groups/individuals who keep up on breaking news, upcoming bills in Congress, and urgent prayer needs. I also maintain several group lists including my "Knee-Buddies," who are my prayer warriors, and I can alert them immediately all at one time. I also use these lists to follow up on regular mail. There*

are many creative ways to use the features of our Internet service providers.

Unsolicited: Some companies buy e-mail lists and bulk mail their advertising to thousands of potential customers within minutes. It's cost effective, they argue, but I maintain that this method does nothing to enhance your company image. Web-sters recognize "junk e-mail" advertising and just click delete.

Save Your Breath: How many times have you repeated your spiel about your business or answered the same question over and over again? On the Internet you can answer all those preliminary questions up front via e-mail, post a Frequently Asked Questions (FAQ) page on your website, or you can type the information, store it in a word processing document, and then just clip and paste it into your e-mail responses. Type it once and use it thousands of times.

Jill: *I get calls, letters, and e-mails with such open-ended questions as "I hear you have a good cooking system. Please tell me about it" and "What is your ministry all about?" I ask them if they have access to the Web. If they do, I politely suggest that they check out our site and tell them that once they've read about our services, I can work with them individually. The response has been terrific. This way we can skip the hours of explaining what we do and how we got started and jump right to specific needs and prayer requests. I calculate that the Web has cut down my snail-mail correspondence by 95 percent, and that translates into quicker response time to others, and into my favorite—more family time.*

One drawback, however, is that e-mail is greatly increased this way, and people expect a quick electronic response.

I also use our site with my speaking ministry. While I'm on the phone with someone who has a separate phone line, they can pull up my site and we go through my onsite publicity kit. This saves days and money. Before I had the site I'd mail out kits that were very costly (4-color, glossy). Now potential hosts can review my schedule, consider my fees, and evaluate my programs immediately. They can print out what they need to present to their committee. I've found my website to be such a blessing. It does most of my paperwork for me, freeing my "work hours" for the actual writing, speaking, counseling, and praying—which is what God called me to do in the first place.

Be creative with your e-mail or website. The possibilities may in fact be endless. I've only begun to give you the whole picture here! A home-business person like you who is trying to work efficiently and juggle family and job may find it a real blessing.

A Professional Site

Before investing in a professional website, ask yourself some questions and learn some keys to good websites.

Defining Your Mission—Set down on paper what you want from a website and what you have to offer surfers. Write out a Web mission statement and your objectives to help you determine if investing your time and money in a website would be worthwhile. Evaluate why being on the Web would be helpful.

Attracting readers—Grabbing online contacts is not as easy as it sounds. Surfers are used to nice-looking sites. They want speedy loading and worthwhile tools when they visit. In other words, unless you're the only one with your product on the planet, with a click of the mouse they'll move to a more attractive or user-friendly site.

Repeats—Web surfers want information. Sites that are just one-page advertisements might get an initial hit, but the Web-ster won't have any reason to return. They recognize "ad"-only sites immediately. You don't want them to only visit once; you want them to move your URL (Universal Resource Locator or website address) to the top of their "favorites" file. Even though updating your site frequently might cost more, it is usually worth the price. You give your visitors a reason to visit each month. Installing a "What's New" section shows them what you've changed. Give away information and provide valuable links to other sources. Offer helpful information or service and they'll return to your site—which is good for business just as repeat store traffic is good for retailers.

Information is the key—Don't be afraid to give free advice. Include an information article about your subject. People are on the Web to get information.

Define "success"—Different people have different ideas about what success means, as I discussed in the last chapter. Pray about what God is doing with your site. One advantage of a website that is well worth considering is how it might impact others for our Lord. You never know when someone surfing will come across your site, see your Christian testimony, and have God use it to touch his or her life in some way. Not every business investment can be measured by the bottom-line!

Let me share the best source I found while I was surfing to double-check my facts for this chapter. Dr. Ralph R. Wilson (www. wilsonweb.com) posts many helpful articles that can help you work out your own Web needs. His e-mail newsletter *Web Commerce Today* is well worth checking out and using. You can subscribe very easily via his website.

Choosing and Contracting with a Web Designer

If you decide that you want more than just e-mail, that you want a home page or a professional website, then you have some more decisions to make. A simple first step is the creation of a home page. Many service providers offer a one-page home page with their standard package. Some even include the homepage design program as part of their package. Developing that kind of page is just a matter of downloading the program, answering a few questions, and composing a few sentences to describe your company and services. You can then link your page to other sites and have a Web presence with only a few hours of work.

Self-Designed or Professional—When you are ready to branch out into a professional website (interactive capability and more than one screen full of matter), decide if you want to design it yourself using more advanced programs or if you want to hire a professional Web designer. Doing it yourself may save dollars up front, but it might cost more in the long run if, because you may be less skilled in Web design, you lose potential customers who get frustrated on their first attempt to visit your site. Simply put, hiring a professional might be worth every penny.

How to Hire a Web Designer—One of the best ways to find a designer is to survey sites and note who is designing the sites you like. Most designers will add a note on the bottom of a home page giving their address. If they are already designing sites similar to what you are interested in, ask them for more information. Also, contact the site hosts for their opinion of their Web designer. Collect data and prices and shop around until you find someone who can work with you, your budget, and your plan. Depending on the Web designer, you'll want to get quotes and a written contract. Be specific about what you want. Websites differ and what you call "a fully-integrated site" might mean something else to a designer. Also ask for fees for each aspect of your site. (For instance, there might be extra charges for a guest registry or each additional page.) Some designers charge by the hour while others quote for the whole package. Prices vary drastically, so you will want to check around.

Bells and Whistles: Website Options

Just as vehicles range from sedans to semis, so do websites. You might choose a simple one-page site just to have a presence, or an elaborate site with multipages, surveys, within-site links, guest registries, and shopping cart capabilities—or anything in between.

Site Access—It's easy and not that costly to register your own domain name. These are much simpler for people to remember and identify. If you choose the less expensive route of using a server, realize that the more letters and slashes people have to remember and type, the less likely they are to log on. I've found that registering a domain name is worth every penny.

Guest Registry—Establishing a registry can be a real benefit as you build a database of possible clients. You can include a quick survey to help you better understand your market. Besides getting names and addresses, you might want to include questions about interests or family size—whatever you need to know to refine your tactics and improve your business. Ask your designer about private registry options. Some sites print all guests' comments, giving you instant endorsements from satisfied customers. But since some guests like their privacy, give them that option by inviting them to contact you via e-mail. Also ask your designer about building into the programming a thank-you note that is automatically sent to each person who registers, a feature which saves hours of work. Automatic mailing list management also saves you the time involved in maintaining your own e-mailing list. You can use this list to alert your visitors of site changes and invite them to come back for a fresh look.

Interactive, video, movement, sound—Some sites offer full-motion video or audio clips. Sometimes the graphics move (for example, flags wave as you read). You'll have to work out these details with your site designer. Keep in mind that, as a courtesy to surfers, these kinds of memory-hungry tricks need an option button and a note of how many bytes they are. This information lets your visitors choose whether or not to load them. In our own surfing, we've found that we leave a site if it starts to take too long to load, but these multimedia add-ins can be very helpful for some businesses.

Site Movement—Some sites are so disorganized and difficult to move around in that visitors give up and leave, even if the information is good. See that your site has several navigational tools that are easy to understand and use. Some options are "Go to" boxes, color-coding of key words, intra-site links, onsite search engines, indexes, tabs, sectional markings, and a site map.

Archives—One valuable and much-appreciated feature that some sites are adding is the archive. This electronic library stores old information that you had onsite in previous months. If visitors missed a month or didn't find you until now, they can scan the archives for interesting information they missed.

Maintenance and Utilization

Admittedly getting the site up and running in the first place calls for the biggest investment of time and money. Once it is up and a pattern of use develops, upkeep should be easy. Set up a schedule for regular changes. Work with your designer about deadlines so you don't put impossible demands on him or her. Continue to expand links from other sites to yours. Surf the Web yourself and, when you find a friendly site, ask for a link. Be willing to offer a link when appropriate.

Attract attention to your site. Print the website address on all your stationery (letterhead, business cards) and use it in all e-mail correspondence. Let everyone know about your site and invite them to visit. Ask for suggestions. You'll be amazed by the good ideas that come in.

To Sell or Not to Sell

You'll want to consider whether to try to make a sale on the site (take orders) or just use it to generate interest and respond to information requests. You'll have to find what works best for you and your product/service. How are you making sales apart from the Internet? Is your product/concept easily understood, or do you usually have to make several contacts before your customers buy? When the Internet was new, most Web-sters were concerned about security and therefore leery about direct buying online. Now with secure sites, credit card numbers are at less risk of theft than when you hand that piece of plastic to total strangers in restaurants and at gas stations, yet we do that every day without thinking about it.

Despite increased security on the Web, the goal of some businesses is simply to generate catalog requests and to give out their toll-free telephone numbers. They don't actually sell anything online. Instead, they view their Internet contacts as prospects only.

Others print their catalogs on-site, complete with an order form that the customers are instructed to print out and mail in with their payments.

With the advent of online stores and secure sites, more and more businesses are taking orders via the Net.

Shopping carts are convenient (and sometimes cute) electronic means for people to work their way through your online store and pick up items for one "ring-out."

Malls are the electronic version of actual shopping malls. For instance, craft malls with dozens of stores (links to websites or to pages of individual craft stores) sell craft projects or supplies for crafters. You might want to explore this option. Just like the big mall in your town, these malls benefit from the group-shopping mentality. Make buying your product/service convenient. Be where shoppers are.

Finally, realize that businesses can benefit from technology that makes the information customers type in at your site hacker-proof. Though it is a popular storyline for science-fiction writers, hacker invasion of your site is not very realistic. If someone is smart enough to get into your secure files, they're smart enough to recognize that they can make more off the big guys than from your sale of hand-crocheted Christmas ornaments.

Possible Hazards

Now let me address a few areas of concern about dealing with the Internet.

Off-Limits Areas: Certain areas of the Internet feed people's sin nature. But just as you don't totally avoid reading because some people publish pornography, you don't have to avoid the Internet because some people are transmitting filth. Learn which areas of the Net to avoid just as you've learned which areas of town not to shop in or visit. Don't search for suggestive words or look for topics that are suspect. Read summaries before clicking to a site. Use links from sites you trust. Choose your forums wisely and know which services demand that sites and chat rooms remain rated G or risk having the plug pulled. Use common sense—always monitor your children's access and use a good filter program.

Web Addiction: Some people have gotten out of control and are unable to limit the time they spend on the Internet. They like the Web too much and are surfing instead of spending time with their families. If you have a home business, you don't have time to become addicted to the Web. Decide to just get on, look up information, do research, answer your mail, and get off. You'll have more, not less, time for your family.

So there you have it. A quick tour of the Web and what it offers business owners like you!

Designing Your Website

Carmen Leal is the author of *WriterSpeaker.com* and *You Can Market Your Book,* as well as two books written for and about people with Huntington's Disease. Carmen knows more about marketing, web design, and using the Internet than about anyone I know. She and her husband, Gary, have a home-based Web design business (WriterSpeaker.com), so the following article* by Carmen is written from both a strong knowledge base and experience.

❧ ❧ ❧

Website Design
by *Carmen Leal*

If a site would be a useful addition to your marketing plan, you need to determine how best to make it happen. Creating a Web site is not rocket science, but there is a learning curve. There

---

* Taken from Carmen Leal, *You Can Market Your Book* (Phoenix: Write Now Publications, 2003), pp. 171-79. Used by permission.

are do-it-yourself books and sites that can either help or confuse, and any number of site designers who would love to help you.

In between those two options is doing it yourself. A good number of you are not technologically inclined and taking on the challenge of creating your own site might be more than you care to handle.

If you do decide to do it yourself, there are many tools that can help. In the resource section at the end of this article…I've listed Web sites that can help you as you begin the process.

WYSIWYG (pronounced WIZ-ee-wig), is an acronym for the phrase *what you see is what you get.* A WYSIWYG editor (program) allows you to create a Web page that lets you see what the end result will look like while the interface or document is being created. A WYSIWYG editor is a quick way to create a site without learning HTML. HTML stands for hypertext markup language. It really is a simple programming language compared to other more robust ones, but it still takes time to learn.

Newer versions of Netscape and Microsoft® Word come equipped with a WYSIWYG if you don't want to spend additional money on software. After reading the product reviews, you can decide if investing in a stand-alone editor makes sense for you.

Beatrice Gormley decided she needed a Web site and, after trying to work with a volunteer Webmaster, went another route. She's not alone in what she's dealt with as I've heard variations of her story from many authors. "My first Web site was set up for me a few years ago as a favor by my husband's nephew's wife. I liked my site, and I got a lot of compliments on it; but I became increasingly frustrated at not being able to update the site myself. For every little thing, I'd have to send the changes—text and any new pictures—to my Webmaster and wait for her to get around to making them. It could take months to get a page about a new book on my site."

Beatrice goes on to share how unacceptable it was to wait for changes to be made. She wanted a tutorial from the Webmaster; but with one in Massachussetts and the other in Colorado, that never happened. As with many Webmasters, this wasn't her day job, so Beatrice's site got pushed further and further down her list of priorities. Hoping that offering to pay for the job would help, she did so.

"I felt uneasy about this and offered to pay her, asking her to tell me what her fees were. She just said she was glad to manage the site for me—and if I'd like to send her a check from time to time to contribute to the cost of the software, that would be great. So I did send her a check from time to time, but I never knew whether it was enough, too much, or stingy."

Things went from bad to worse when her Webmaster became her husband's nephew's ex-wife. Eventually Beatrice decided something had to give if she wanted an up-to-date Web site.

"When the Authors Guild, to which I've belonged for years, began offering Web site hosting, complete with a user-friendly site builder (no need for me to learn HTML code), it sounded exactly like what I wanted. By this time I had my own fax/scanner, so I could scan book covers and photos that I wanted to put on my site."...

Many [people] have chosen to work with someone already well versed in creating Web sites, rather than investing a lot of time in learning a new skill. When I teach at writers' conferences, I am often asked how much an average site should cost. There are too many variables to give you an average cost; but like any service, it pays to do your homework before spending your money.

I recommend making lists of sites you like, both author sites and others, and sending an e-mail to the site owners. A few questions might be all it takes to find the right designer for you. Ask them who designed their site and if they were happy with the service; who came up with the design; who provided the graphics; how long it took; and, if they are willing to tell you, how much it cost. If they are willing to share the cost, find out if it costs extra for maintenance.

Once you have several designers to choose from, send them an e-mail message, inquiring about their services and rates. Visit their Web sites and learn as much as possible about the way they do business. Ask them for a minimum of three clients you can e-mail and ask the above questions. Regardless of who you hire, always ask for a contract.

My husband, a Web designer and programmer with over twenty-five years experience, specializes in creating sites for writers and speakers. We have an all-inclusive package that works well....You're welcome to visit our design site at www.writerspeaker.com/design. html and read our contract and use it as a guideline for whatever designer you hire.

A Web site is more than pretty pictures and text pulled together for visitors to see. Once you have determined your site's focus and goals, you have a starting place. Site design includes not only the look and feel, but also the functionality. When my husband, Gary, designs or evaluates a site for clients, they work together to create a unique look that incorporates the author's personality and mission.

Besides the basic attractiveness of a site, Gary makes sure the site is functional and easy for visitors to find. A few months ago I heard about a new novel with Huntington's Disease in the plot line. I wanted to communicate with the author and offer to do a book review for him, so I did a search to find his Web site. I searched for close to an hour. Although I found his book listed on many Web sites and bookstores, I couldn't find his personal site.

I finally wrote to his publisher, asking for an e-mail or Web site address for him and received his site address. After a quick look at his site, I knew exactly why I couldn't find it in a search. It was obvious the author had paid a professional to create the site, and it was attractive. The navigation was fine, and there was lots of information. There was also a big problem. The designer had made the site as an image map. Instead of being a combination of text and pictures written in code that was easily indexed by search engines, the designer had simply taken all the components and made one large image. The author had a Web site; but unless you knew the address, you couldn't find it because search engines don't index image maps.

Web Site Basics

It's impossible to give you everything you need to know to design a site. Instead, what I've tried to do is give you guidelines to get you started. In addition to the suggestions listed below, there's a ten-point site evaluation worksheet on my Web site that will help you or someone you hire put together an effective site.

As you get started, follow these guidelines:

- Your site should have a clear, easily recognizable focus.

- The information should be easy to find and easy to use.

- The design should be appealing to its intended audience....

- Backgrounds should not overwhelm the text. Pictures and graphics should be of the highest quality possible, and any animated graphics should have a specific purpose and not be distracting.

- The site navigation system should be obvious, and visitors should be able to easily find their way around the site.

- The content should be well-organized and broken into categories versus being on one or two long pages. Every page should be user friendly, and all links should work. The content should be well written and give visitors a reason to make repeat visits.

- The design should reflect your personality, mission, and brand and be appropriate for the intended audience.

- To ensure that all pages load as quickly as possible, all graphics should be sized and optimized for speed.

- A link to the contact information should be found easily on each page.

- Your site should be constructed to be easily indexed by search engines. A variey of well-chosen description and meta tags should be included on all pages. Unless you or a professional designer understands how to program for indexibility, avoid using frames or image maps.

It's important to remember that creating and maintaining a Web site is a process. Later you can add links to other sites of value to your readers, a search engine, a subscription newsletter or e-zine, new content, and other items to enhance your site.

Whoever designs your site should view each page on both a PC and a Mac, using different versions of both Netscape and Internet Explorer. Not everyone uses your operating system or browser; and pages may look different, depending on the browser, operating system, and settings. Finding out how your pages look to others will help you create a more universal site.

Another thing to remember is that even if you choose fonts to create the look and feel that's right for you, not everyone has those fonts. By adding a common default font, you have more control over how your site looks to those who don't have your preferred font.

Regardless of your topic and specific design, the content must be easily understood and deemed valuable to your target audience. Obviously your writing needs to be gramatically correct, properly punctuated, and spelled correctly....

Include adequate information and links to make visitors feel the site is worth recommending to others. I've seen too many sites that mix up content and end up trying to meet the needs of many people, but come across as disjointed.

I now have three unique sites, each with its own distinctive, yet related, look and feel. A link to the other sites is featured on each page, but the content on each is original. The site to promote this book *[You Can Market Your Book]* and *WriterSpeaker.com* has information about my books, of course; but it also has articles and links for writers and speakers. My company site has a focus on Huntington's

Disease and my other nonwriting speaking topics, and I have a third site to promote our quotation management software.

Putting up the page is easy, making sure it's maintained with new content added on a regular basis is time consuming. It's also effective.

Naming Your Site

In most cases your name or your business name is the perfect choice for a domain name. If your name is already taken, you can always use your middle initial or go with .net or .org instead of .com. If for some reason you decide to use a name other than your own, remember that choosing the right domain name for your Web site is essential if you want an effective site.

The name should explain what your site contains and, equally if not more important, it should be a common word, so people can remember it easily. Choose a name that will also serve as a keyword for the site, so the search engines will show it when people search for sites like yours.

Graphics

Besides making your page slow to load and possibly irritating, there's another reason to avoid too many graphics. Search engines read only text and images, and a page with too many graphics and little text is almost negligible to a search engine. There are ways to design a graphics-heavy page more efficiently, and a good designer will know the tricks. But the best way to make sure your graphics aren't a hindrance and to make a pleasing page is to use balance between the two.

A Search-Engine Friendly Site

I've stressed the importance of content, but in reality the most important words on your site aren't seen by your visitors. A description tag is a concise sentence or two used to describe your site. This is what is seen in the search result when your site comes up after someone does a search on Yahoo, Google, or another search engine. If there is no description tag present, the first text on your first page will be what the reader sees as a site description.

Keywords are a type of shorthand used by search engines to index your page. They describe your page and what makes it unique and different from others on the Web. The words you select should also appear throughout the text on various pages. Make sure they appear in main headings and section headers. Also plan your paragraphs, so keywords appear somewhere in the introduction, content, and conclusion sentences.

Keywords should be as specific as possible. If you must use popular keywords because that's what your page is about, combine them with other words to make phrases that people might search for. Your keywords can be single words or two- or three-word phrases separated by a comma. Also use a few synonyms of the keyword in your text. The idea is to use keywords that are common enough so the typical searcher might use them, but unique enough to avoid millions of pages being returned in a search result.

Search engines ignore the most common words. These are called "stop words" because the engines don't bother to stop to read them. They typically ignore adjectives and articles, so don't rely on them as critical keywords on your page.

If no one can find your site using search engines, then you limit not only possible sales, but the impact you can make in people's lives. The best way to get higher search-engine placement is by registering your own domain name. At the end of this section are several domain registration and hosting companies where you can find low prices and excellent service.

To ensure your site gets consistently high search-engine rankings, develop excellent content, then people will be more likely to return to your site and encourage others to visit. The more traffic your site has, the higher you rise in the pecking order.

I'll conclude with two final words of caution. Whether you design a site yourself or hire a professional, make sure you keep a written record of your hosting company, user name, and password.

We have had the unfortunate experience of an author not being able to access his site to make changes because he didn't have his user name or password, and the person who set up the site has disappeared.

The other caution is to make sure your e-mail address is current with the registration company. Renewal notices are sent to the e-mail on record; and if you have changed your account, the notice will never reach you. Many domain names have been claimed by someone else because people didn't know it was time to renew. Make sure you know your domain's expiration date and that you renew it at least thirty days in advance, so there's no confusion and you keep your identity.

Before you start creating what has the potential to be one of your most powerful marketing tools, study other sites. Keep it simple, easy to navigate, and interactive. Your home page should be where you spend the majority of your time and effort and consider your site visitors every step of the way.

Last of all, a Web site is only one way to market, so pace yourself. As you begin or continue the design process, don't neglect other opportunities.

❧ ❧ ❧

Recommended Resources
Domain Registration

    GoDaddy   www.godaddy.com

Hosting Services

    Author's Den (free)   www.authorsden.com
    Authors Guild (fee)   www.authorsguild.com
    Christian Web Host (fee)   www.christianwebhost.com
    ChurchSites (fee)   www.churchsites.com

Cornerstone Hosting (fee)   www.cornerstonehosting.com
Flock Hosting   www.flockhosting.com
FutureQuest (fee)   www.futurequest.com
Half Price Hosting (fee)   www.halfprice.com
HomewithGod (free)   www.homewithgod.com
Our Church (free)   www.ourchurch.com
Truepath (free & fee)   www.truepath.com
Wolf Digital   www.wolfdigital.net/hosting.htm

Association

The Christian Webmaster's
Association   http://cweb.gospelcom.net

WYSIWYGs

About.com   http://webdesign.about.com/
                             compute/webdesign/msubeditors.
                             htm

Web Site Tools

Bravenet   www.bravenet.com
C/NET   www.cnet.com/software/0-8172.
                             7-309066.html
Pico Search Engine   www.picosearch.com
Search Engine Registration   www.uxn.com/search_engines.html
The Chicken's Guide
to Site Promotion   www.guide.bloonatic.com*

---

* Used by permission of Carmen Leal.

Telecommuting

Starting your own home business is certainly not the only way to be home-based. Instead, many people who want to combine traditional job security, a regular paycheck, and company benefits with home-based employment do so by telecommuting and working for an employer from home. Here's how one woman left the corporate office for a home office without starting a business of her own.

Gail loved her job as a publicist for a major recording house, and she had worked hard for three years to earn that position. For five years she worked at the job of her dreams, and then God answered another one of her prayers. She was pregnant. She and her husband discussed their options, and full-time daycare was not one of them. "I know I can do my job from home," she told her husband. "I go into my office, I get on the phone, and I work on my computer. About the only time I see other employees is at break time." However, no one who had worked in-house at her company had ever switched to working from home, and Gail knew her chances were slim.

But Gail prepared a written proposal outlining how her employer would benefit, how she would benefit, and, in order of her preference, four options for her employer to choose from. "I told them that I didn't want to quit and that I could 1) work from home 40 hours a week; 2) work three days a week in the office and two days at home; 3) work in the office from 8-2; or 4) work 8-2 in the office and the other ten hours at home. Unfortunately, they thought the home options would never work and agreed to number three. I walked out of that meeting agreeing to work 30 hours in the office to keep my benefits, yet I still didn't feel good about the decision. Even though I'd offered those options, I had a knot in my stomach as I realized, 'I will have my child in daycare everyday. I'm putting extra income ahead of my child.'"

She poured her heart out to her husband, and they agreed that, even though they were saving to purchase their first home, she would quit. About a month later, she went in to resign. Her supervisor asked her what she really wanted to do, and Gail immediately replied, "Do my job out of my home." So she prepared a second proposal, hoping they would value her five years of experience enough to agree. Gail knew she was risking her job at that point, but she was prepared for that risk and ready to lose her position if necessary. Instead, her employer agreed to allow her to work 35 hours a week from her home, enough to keep all of her benefits.

Although an adjustment, the at-home arrangement has worked well. Gail works from 8 to 2 and then closes her office door. She puts in her last hour of the day at night when she reads, and she goes into the company office for an hour for a weekly meeting. "I had a system for doing my work at the corporate office, and I try to stick to that. I spend my mornings on the phone, do correspondence in the afternoon, and finish up in the evenings when it's quiet. During breaks and in the afternoon, I get to play with my child." How does the company benefit? Sometimes they get more than 35 hours a week, and she's proved to her supervisor that her productivity has increased now that she's home-based.

If you think that you, like Gail, could do your current job from your home, consider her advice. "Seriously and professionally, make your proposal to your boss. If you never ask, you'll never get anywhere. Being able to walk away from your job gives you an advantage, although not everyone can do that. Present your value to the company. You are a benefit to them, so don't sell yourself short. If you leave, they'll have to find applicants to replace you, narrow the field and interview them, and spend time and money training someone. Emphasize how the company would benefit from your arrangement."

Gail agrees that, while it does look like she has the best of both worlds, it's not the easiest road to take. Still, the emotional benefit and peace of mind of being available for her child is her motivation. "You're a valuable employee, but you're more valuable to your child than to your job. If, as a Christian, you're putting your child first because you feel that's what God has called you to do, then you can believe that God will meet your needs. He has for me."

What has Gail's employer thought of the arrangement?

Gail's supervisor says that Gail did three things that made her proposal to work from home successful. First, she had already proven herself an extremely organized, self-motivated, and loyal employee in the office. Second, she realistically evaluated the job functions she could do at home. Third, she showed her flexibility and willingness to find workable solutions by presenting several options to her company. "Gail applies a determined, goal-oriented attitude toward everything she does, and I knew her attitude toward telecommuting would be no different. She has proven she can complete her projects at home and keep our clients well-served. However, while Gail is able to accomplish as much, or even more, at home, her physical absence leaves a leadership void that isn't as tangible. Even though she makes herself available by phone, some everyday questions and problems that used to go to her are absorbed by others in the department. And long-distance communication is always harder for both parties than face-to-face communication, so it takes an extra commitment between workers still in the office and those at home.

"If you are considering telecommuting, remember that every work situation will have its plusses and minuses. When presenting a telecommuting proposal to your company, step back and try to honestly read the proposal as if you were the owner of the company.

What drawbacks are there for this employee in working from home? What benefits will the company receive? If you've presented your case well, the benefits should outweigh the drawbacks."

Telecommuting or working from home part- or full-time for an employer is a viable option for those who want to stay on the company payroll yet be at home. Telecommuters stay connected with their company through phone, e-mail, and fax. Many people love the idea of telecommuting because it gives them an opportunity to forgo the traffic and to work at home without the risk of starting up a business. One telecommuter said, "At home my office is large, I have a good computer and printer, and even the coffee is better. As long as people are productive, companies should let people work at home."[1]

The latest in affordable technology has enabled unprecedented numbers of people to work for others from their own home. With standard office equipment becoming the home-office standard, opportunities to telecommute are growing. It is becoming ever more popular as companies clamor to find new ways to work and as employees search for new ways to integrate work with family life. Many workers can do their jobs at home on a full-time or part-time basis as an independent contractor for someone else, an option that is good to know about if entrepreneurship or telecommuting isn't your cup of tea.

A man from Boise, Idaho, decided to change his life when he set up a computer, a phone line, a modem, a printer, and a facsimile machine in a spare bedroom. Instead of fighting traffic in the morning, he now reads his e-mail and checks in with his company by computer before 8:00 A.M. This telecommuter isn't alone. It's difficult to track the numbers of telecommuters but some say there were 19.6 million people in 1999[2] and possibly 29 million people in 2003[3] who engaged in some telework.

Many small companies have adopted casual work-at-home programs. Some large corporations, however, have adopted a formal telecommuting program. One company changed its personnel policy to allow mothers who have had children within the last three years to do some work at home. A telecommuting pilot program in California from 1988–1990 found an average sick leave reduction of 19 percent and derived a financial benefit to the employer of $3,815 per telecommuter. The Los Angeles County program reported the productivity jumped 34 percent among clerical workers who code documents at home.

Working at home for others is also a viable option for the disabled, the handicapped, single parents, mothers who want extended maternity leave, and many retired people who still want to work. Since people are living longer and retiring earlier, this segment of the population is growing rapidly. Some companies are actively trying to hire retired persons. Some are even offering personal computer training.

Both companies and employees can benefit from a telecommuting program. The companies don't have to pay overhead for these employees, turnover can be cut down, and productivity can be increased by as much as 20 to 60 percent. Some companies can expand without increasing physical space by letting employees go home. For a short time I worked for a company that did this. I was working half my time at the office and half my time at home. When new employees were added, space became scarce, so I jumped at the chance to work strictly at home. I was still an employee, still got my paycheck every Friday, and still had my company benefits. In fact, that very situation eventually led me to my own home business.

Many jobs—from data entry to actually running a company—can be done just as well at home as they can in the office. Salaried home-based workers often include accountants, salespeople, researchers, bookkeepers, writers, insurance agents, data entry personnel, lawyers, artists, stockbrokers, telemarketing representatives, word processors, and many others.

Telecommuting works best when people have jobs where productivity can be measured, but many companies still need to break the "I must see my employees to effectively manage them" mindset.

Even when managers have difficulty supervising absent employees, the quality of the work those employees produce will indicate whether they are working at home effectively. But if, for your boss's sake, you need to punch a time clock for him or her to know whether you are giving your all, you will have trouble. If your boss or corporation cannot see past the time card to what your output is, telecommuting will be difficult. Surveys have found that telecommuting is also difficult for people whose jobs mean they must deal directly with people in a managerial capacity, attend frequent meetings, or work on computers tied to mainframes, as well as for those in purchasing or building management.[4]

Gil Gordon Associates, www.gilgordon.com has founded a business based on the telecommuting trend. He consults with organizations to help them implement telecommuting programs and says that most companies select telecommuters from within their current in-office workforce. Telecommuting employers look for people who possess some of the same characteristics as entrepreneurs. They want people who can meet their deadlines, are disciplined, and are self-motivated. They want their employees to have worked out childcare arrangements and to have enough space at home to do the work. They are also looking for people who do not need the social atmosphere of the office environment to be happy in their work.

If you want to work at home for someone else, consider this:

- First, look for a type of job that's not time-dependent—a job that can be done during the day or night whenever you have the time available.

- Second, set a realistic goal about the number of hours you can actually work. Depending on the age and number of your children, this can vary from full-time to just a few hours a week. Gordon says, "A lot of people have been burned by setting unrealistic expectations for themselves. Ask yourself, 'How late do I want to stay up at night doing this?'" When you're burning the midnight oil for someone else, it's easy to get resentful. Determine beforehand just how much you want to work.

• Third, consider the availability of another childcare provider, whether your spouse, your grandma, or a neighbor. When you work for other people you are subject to their demands, and most employers prefer that the childcare issue not hinder your work for them. Working at home for someone else while raising children can be more trying than working for yourself because you have someone other than yourself to please. Bosses expect a certain quota and quality of work. If you do not meet their expectations because you're juggling your kids and your work, you won't be working for them very long. If you're going to be working full-time, decide before you start what kind of childcare help you will have. Doing two full-time jobs at once means that neither job gets your best.

Ways to Work at Home for Others

1. *Approach your current or former employer.* If you have a good track record and your job can be done at home, you may be able to negotiate a work-at-home position. Prove yourself as an employee and volunteer to take special projects or part of your work home occasionally. Let management see the effectiveness of this method. You might propose working at home on an extended project or for part of your work week. When you have demonstrated that you can do your job effectively from home, then propose your work-at-home plan to your boss. If you are not employed or your present job cannot be done at home begin looking for another salaried position that might be done from home and try to sell a new employer on your idea. Tell as many people as you can that you are looking for this type of work.

2. *Look for a subcontracting arrangement.* A subcontractor works at home without owning his own business. If you don't have a current or former employer with which to establish a work-at-home arrangement, how do you find the companies that are doing this? Gil Gordon says, "Shoe leather research!" As a rule, companies do not advertise work-at-home positions, so tell people that you are looking for a subcontracting arrangement. Talk with business owners in the field in which you want to work. Try to get a feel for who is doing the type of work you are interested in and who might need some help.

Check out available resources, such as *The Work-at-Home Sourcebook* by Lynie Arden, which lists companies that have telecommuting programs and describes how to find such jobs.

The continued growth of home-based work depends a lot on how businesses respond. Hopefully more and more companies will see the potential of using home-based workers who are full-fledged employees of their corporations. The future of successful telecommuting programs rests in the hands of employees and company decision-makers. Employees should continue to lobby for the work-at-home option, proposing formal or informal programs to their employers. Company executives should discover what many other progressive companies already have—that having employees telecommute and do part-time or full-time work from home is not only viable, but beneficial to the company as well as the employee.

Employees Versus Independent Contractors

If you work for someone else at home, be careful of the way in which you are paid and treated by your employer. Are you an employee or an independent contractor? Many companies treat their workers as employees but pay them as independent contractors. You are an employee if someone other than you controls how and when you work. You are an independent contractor if you decide the terms of your work arrangements and can work for more than one company. (Some contract consultants, who consult with one company for a period of time, are limited to working strictly for that company for the duration of their contract, but are then free to take on new clients.)

A plumber might be an independent contractor. He might have his own tools, call his own shots, decide how to do the work, and have multiple clients. Compare that to someone who does word processing at home 30 or 40 hours a week for the same word-processing bureau. That agency assigns the work, tells the worker how to do it, checks his work, and sets his rate of pay. That person is an employee. However, if that word-processing person worked for someone who allowed him to work at home if he wanted to, to work for others, to accept or turn down jobs at will without jeopardizing his position, and to work his own hours and in his own way, then for all practical purposes he would be an independent contractor.

Some people don't mind being paid on a contract basis. They have nothing taken out of their checks, so they get more money on the front end. Sometimes both parties are happy with this arrangement, but the IRS has said that it doesn't matter to what the two parties agree. The danger is not necessarily that home-workers are going to be exploited and paid less than a traditional worker, since some home-workers say they are earning as much as or more than their office counterparts on a per-hour basis. However, they are not getting the matching contributions from Social Security, the unemployment insurance coverage, or, in some cases, worker's compensation protection. Not only could the employer get into trouble for this, but it's benefit money out of the pockets of the workers—today's money as well as their retirement income. Since the employer is not matching the Social Security payments, that employee pays a higher percentage than the amount that would be deducted from his or her paycheck.

Beware of Fraudulent Home-Working Opportunities

Many ads in newspapers and magazines, the Internet, and signs posted around town promise the moon for the price of peanuts:

"Home-Workers Wanted: Big Profits. No Experience" or "Envelope Stuffing. Big Money." Think about it—would employers really let others in on big profits without either experience or an investment? Here's how one of the schemes work: People place those phony ads looking for people who want to work at home and strike it rich. You just "send $15 for more information." What you receive in return are details on how to set up a business like theirs, defrauding other people. You would then invest in stamps, envelopes, and other items and buy advertisements inviting other unsuspecting people to send you money "for more information." In these schemes, there is no actual job at issue.

In other schemes, people propose to pay you a certain amount for each envelope you stuff for them. You must then buy their fliers and pay for your own ads that ask others to send you a self-addressed stamped envelope for more information on how to earn money at home. After you receive a certain quota of these envelopes, you stuff them and give them to your employer for payment. This type of job requires you to spend your own funds, and payment depends on the number of responses to your ads—not a great way to make a living!

The U.S. Postal Service Investigation Service has said, "In practically all businesses, envelope stuffing has become a highly mechanized operation using sophisticated mass mailing techniques and equipment which eliminates any profit potential for an individual doing this type of work at home. The Inspection Service knows of no work-at-home promotion that ever produces income as alleged."[5] That Service, incidentally, put more than 3,500 of these fraudulent operations out of business! Other ads for home-based work ask you to send money, but all you may get is a list of firms that use home-workers. You must then contact each firm individually.

The old saying that "if it sounds too good to be true, it probably is" holds true for home-working advertisements. If the ad asks you to send money, beware. Investigate before you invest. Do a little research. See if the company's phone number is listed with directory assistance and call to see if anyone answers during business hours. If you have questions, call the Better Business Bureau in your area and in the city listed in the ad. If you are (or suspect you are) a victim of mail fraud, write to Mail Fraud, Chief Postal Inspector, Postal Inspection Services, Washington, D.C. 20260, or to the Postal Inspector in care of the city in the ad.

Some reputable mass-mailing companies may hire home-workers, but get these leads from the Yellow Pages, not the classifieds. Don't send money and be sure there's a local phone number, not just a post office box number.

Take-Out Work

Many people who have traditional office jobs also spend some time at home working for their employers. According to studies, people do this so-called take-out work to avoid interruptions, to meet deadlines, to make up for lack of time at the office, and to be with their family more often. Companies often help employees by purchasing or helping them purchase equipment to enable them to do some take-out work.

Bill Mattox, formerly of the Family Research Council, says, "I think one of the things we like to be encouraging is not only more home-based work, where people work almost exclusively out of the home in some type of business, but also more take-out work, where workers who have families want to organize their lives around their family's schedule rather than organizing their family schedules around work."

Bringing the Workplace into Your Home

Living and working in the same location can be both a blessing and a curse. While the blessings are numerous, there is also great potential for mass chaos. Imagine what it would be like if a Fortune 500 company president decided to start sleeping at the office to get more accomplished. He's a man with an important job, and he doesn't want to spend wasted time commuting. He brings in his sleeping bag, toiletries, and some personal articles. Gradually more and more of his belongings make their way in. He misses his family so they begin to visit him all the time. By now his office is strewn with his personal belongings, looking very unprofessional, and his work papers are sharing space with his electric skillet and toothbrush. The family and the dog are now permanently residing at his office as well. This man with the important job is now up to his neck in alligators. Chaos reigns, and he's getting little done. His office doesn't look like or even function like an office anymore because *home has invaded work!*

Likewise, work can overtake your home. Your tranquil domicile opens up its doors to a business endeavor, the home business takes off, and now your orderly belongings and lovely decor are cohabitating with a sleeping giant—your business.

You are a woman with important jobs—being a wife, mother, homemaker, and now businesswoman. But the business has invaded your domestic retreat. The phone rings off the wall. A steady stream of people pop in continually and at a moment's notice. Your work papers are keeping the dining room table buried. Your laundry is in a big heap because, while your work paraphernalia is abundant, your time is not. You can't get anything done. Your house doesn't look like or even function like your house anymore because *work has invaded your home!*

This second scene isn't pure fiction. I know because I've been there. Other home-workers have also experienced that same feeling of home/work chaos. Yet it doesn't have to be like that. With proper planning and a commitment to do all things as unto the Lord, you can live in entrepreneurial domestic tranquillity.

How? What are the main problems in this area, and how can you avoid them? Let's look.

Keeping Home Life from Invading Work

Let's start with the problem of running a successful business in a home amid its paraphernalia and its occupants. You want to be professional. You want to get as much done in as little time as possible. But you and I face some problems that our office-residing business counterparts do not have to tackle.

Problem number 1: You succumb to the "I can't get it all done" syndrome. If you think for a millisecond that you can run your home efficiently, run your business well, and be supermom without delegating some of your tasks, you'd better think again. The best business managers are those who delegate things that do not need their direct involvement. As a home-business owner you can delegate jobs in your business, jobs in your home, or both, depending on the amount of your work and the degree of help you get. You may need help with the housework, help with the children, help with your business, or any combination thereof. Recognize when you do need help and then take action to get it. Attempts at being a supermom don't do you, your family, or your business any good. For specifics on this, see chapter 12 on managing your home.

Problem number 2: You can't mentally divorce yourself from your home surroundings, thereby making it difficult to get started or to concentrate on your work. People with "traditional" jobs who drive to their place of business don't have to look at a mess all day long if they leave their homes in a state of chaos. The home-business person cannot afford to do this; he or she is stuck with looking at and working in the mess. This is extremely distracting. While some people are very good at blocking out the unsightly array of their home, I am not. If the beds aren't made, dirty dishes sit in the sink, and my den looks like Toys-Я-Us, I find it extremely difficult to settle in for a productive morning's work. I may start working, but pretty soon I let a phone call interruption become an excuse for a quick break to make the bed. If I have a particularly busy afternoon, I may stop again and quickly wash the dishes. Working like this is frustrating and counterproductive. By dividing attention between work and the house, I accomplish little in either area.

If you find it easy to work happily and productively in a state of disarray, congratulations. If you don't, make it a habit to pick up things before you begin working. I have found that if I take 30 minutes or so to straighten up in the morning, I get a lot more done during the day because I'm not wondering when I'll have time to get it done. I'm in a better state of mind because my work environment is more pleasant. Besides, if I'm more organized I'm also more productive. Establish a routine that works for *you.*

Even if your house is always as neat as a pin, you may find other things in your home distracting—the photographs under the bed that need organizing, the thank-you cards you need to get mailed, the grocery list you need to write. There are always little projects at home that need your attention. Working in the same place causes you to be reminded of them more than if you worked elsewhere. One woman who runs a typesetting and design business from her home, says, "Juggling priorities is difficult. I have to stay motivated to go out and solicit business. Because I am home, I tend to see things around the house I need to do or things I want to do with my daughter." That is why it is so helpful to have a workplace in your home that is separated from family living areas. It's so much easier to forget about the mess or the projects if you can walk into your home office and shut the door. Even if you don't have a separate room in your home for your business, do as much as you can to make your work area separate.

Problem number 3: How in the world do you run a home business with children underfoot? While having our children around is one of the benefits of home businesses, it is also a problem at times. There's no doubt that small children can make working at home a real challenge. This topic gets its own chapter! See chapter 13: Where Do the Children Fit In? Right now, let me just assure you that it is possible to combine your kids and your business successfully without going bonkers.

Problem number 4: You neglect your work because you find it difficult to alternate your mothering apron with your business hat. It's easy to neglect your work, especially when you love your job of raising the precious little ones that God has given you. But if we spend all our time with the kids or let them and their schedules dictate our lives, we thwart our efforts to succeed in our business. One home-working mom says, "It's easy to fall into being a mother and full-time homemaker and dropping the business because you are at home. You're not removed at an office, where you are away from everything. It's easy to get lazy in your business because you want to spend time with your family." Even without children, it can still be difficult to stick to your work when your spouse is around. If your mate is watching an old movie or tending the barbecue while sipping a glass of lemonade, you may find it tough to concentrate on your task at hand.

The key here is to set hours for yourself and schedule your work time. One home-worker I know works best in the very early hours of the morning, before seeing to the needs of her family. Someone else may work best late at night, setting aside time to work after the kids are in bed. Whatever your schedule and work habits are, you will be more productive if you schedule time each week to get your work done. Then, with work out of the way, you are free to enjoy your family.

Problem number 5: You lose valuable work time to outside forces. The phone rings incessantly. The neighbors drop by. Friends ask favors of you since you're "home during the day." In general, people infringe on your time because you are in a home environment.

People working in an office environment have built-in protection from such outside forces: secretaries, receptionists, and office buildings. Friends aren't as likely to call just to chat when they have to get past the front desk to get to you. The very nature of the office environment discourages a great many outside interruptions.

Working at home is so much "friendlier." People don't usually mean to disturb you, but often they don't understand that you do have to work even though you aren't in an office. They also don't know that their visit or phone call was ill-timed or one in a string of such interruptions.

Many home-workers solve this problem by setting business hours. They make sure that as many people as possible know the usual hours they work. If people know that you usually work in the mornings, or on Tuesdays and Wednesdays, or regular full-time business hours, chances are they'll try to honor your schedule, and you'll get more done. (Answering machines also solve a host of problems; more on that in a minute.)

Problem number 6: You chat too much with friends, make the refrigerator your constant companion, or are otherwise lacking in self-discipline. Many people say they would have difficulty in working at home because they just couldn't stay away from their Kenmore double-doors. Others say they would talk on the phone too much, visit with their neighbors, or watch daytime TV. Those are valid concerns for many people, but the bottom line issue with all of these "work-stoppers" is lack of discipline. You could padlock the fridge or throw out the TV, but if you don't have discipline in your life, working at home will be a source of frustration instead of the joy that it can be.

The Bible tells us to be disciplined. We must strive to achieve this character in our lives in order to be successful home-workers. "Listen to counsel and accept discipline, that you may be wise the rest of your days" (Proverbs 19: 20).

Many home-workers identify some of the problem areas of working at home as snacking, sleeping late, watching TV, talking on the phone, talking with neighbors, reading, becoming too unprofessional, and procrastinating.

If you think that any of these or other temptations in your life might become a problem while you work at home, ask the Lord to build the discipline in your life that is necessary to overcome the obstacles. Not only will this self-discipline help you in your home business, but the overall quality of your life will improve as well. If a bad habit has become excessive in your life, recognize it as such. Knowing that you have a problem with food, TV, or whatever is often the first step toward solving it.

If you have trouble staying away from the kitchen, try scheduling snacks instead of waiting until the urge to eat hits you. (You'll eat healthier this way anyway.) Don't buy junk food, since it's much more tempting to grab a bag of chips to munch at your desk than it is to fix a healthy snack. If TV is a problem, try unplugging it during the day. If you have to go to the trouble of bending down to plug it in and then turn it on, you might stop the habit of just flicking the switch.

Develop good habits from the beginning. Learning to be disciplined in your life is much easier than trying to break a bad habit once it has developed.

Keeping Work from Invading Home Life

It's easy to let this problem get out of hand. I remember one zinger of a week. In my trusty organizer I made out my schedule and had plenty of built-in flextime. I knew what deadlines I had, what business desk-work I needed to tackle, what time to leave for my daughter's field trip. What I hadn't planned on was the volume of interruptions. In four days eight people dropped by unexpectedly. Many of them stayed several hours. On one day alone I received more than 20 phone calls. By the fifth day of this schedule, work was piling up, and I was a bit agitated. I hadn't been able to finish the work I had wanted, my time with my family had been interrupted, and I was frustrated. I had to determine my problem and rethink how I could prevent this. It is too easy to let work dictate your family life.

Problem number 1: The phone keeps ringing. What can you do? Two things: Use an answering machine or get an answering service or voice mail. When you are working and don't want to be interrupted you can let the machine take your calls. Or you can simply screen who you have time to talk to at that moment and then return the calls as soon as it is convenient for you. (You also don't have to miss business calls when you are seeing to the needs of your family.)

Better yet get a business line. This way when the phone rings you know it's a business call and you can answer the phone appropriately. Also, after business hours you will know which calls are personal and which are business. If it's dinner-time with the family and the business line rings, let the machine or voice mail get it.

Many phone companies offer special services, and one that can be invaluable to the home-business operator is a distinctive ring. For a small fee you can have a second phone number—with a distinctive ring—using your current line. If you don't have a very high volume of business calls, you can then use that second ring for business only, and you'll be able to distinguish personal calls from business calls. One writer friend of mine has two separate phone lines, but she also has a distinctive ring on the family line. Only her husband and children have the phone number for that distinctive ring so she can screen calls while she is writing and allow the answering machine to get all the calls except the most important ones. Following her example, you could have up to four phone numbers on only two residential lines and organize your business calls by controlling how you pass out the telephone numbers.

Problem number 2: People needing your "business time" drop in, stay too long, and fragment your time. There is a fine line between being flexible ("going with the flow") and allowing other people to dictate your schedule. Flexibility is important in a home business, but without any structure to your schedule you can be taken advantage of. To help solve this problem, learn to say no and set business hours.

Saying no isn't always easy, but it will save you headaches in your business. I will confess that this truth has been hard for me to learn. When friends call and ask a favor, I want to be available to help them. Telling them no is often difficult, but sometimes necessary. When clients call and need "servicing," it's hard not to say yes immediately. One thing I have learned is to be stringent with my time. After all, the most valuable commodity in any business is the owner's time. So I encourage you to, instead of immediately saying yes when a client or friend calls asking for a meeting or a favor, evaluate the timing.

As Christians, we are called to be Christlike in our family life, our business life, and our personal contacts. Meeting other people's needs—whether by dropping everything to fill a rush order for a client or babysitting for a friend—is one way we serve as Jesus Himself served. Just remember to think through what you say yes to. If agreeing to a business meeting at 10:30 disrupts the timetable for the rest of your day, don't hesitate to suggest something that better fits your schedule. If your time is really short, let people know this, and suggest a starting and ending time for your meeting. They will respect you for your honesty. This is especially helpful if you have clients coming into your home.

Meetings with people outside your home also require tact if you feel they are going on too long and taking up too much of your time. But if these meetings are in your home, ending them can be difficult.

You can't just walk out! If you set up a business meeting in your home, tell your clients in advance what time you have available. Try something like "John, I'd love to meet with you. How about Tuesday from 9 o'clock to 10:15?" If it's a personal visit that's keeping you from work, don't be afraid to let your visitor know that you must get back to your work. (Just do so tactfully!)

If you have set hours (or if people at least think you do), it's easier to control your schedule instead of having it control you. When I was in desktop publishing, I initially had a problem with clients calling or wanting to come by at all hours. Dinner with the family was frequently disturbed. I was called on weekends and late in the evenings. This was ruining my family time, and I felt like I never had any time off. I was always "on call" with my business. I finally learned to simply tell my clients my business hours and ask them to please call me or set appointments during those times. They didn't mind, and my family life improved significantly.

Problem number 3: Business visitors complicate your home life. A trick that one home-worker uses is to encourage those who do business with her to drop off or pick up items even when she is not there. That allows her business to continue, in a sense, while she is away. I do this quite frequently myself. Just agree on a safe place outside your home for the item to be left. One home-worker sets a box outside for her customers to drop off their work during her off hours. Be cautious, however, of potential problems like bad weather or theft.

If business guests pose a problem at your home, try also doing business by mail, fax, telephone, or computer as often as possible. Offer to go to their location or to meet somewhere centrally located (perhaps a restaurant). Some of these situations may take you away from your home more often than you like, so determine what makes your home/work life easier for you.

Problem number 4: Deadlines rob you of family time. This is one of the hardest problems to avoid in many businesses. Have the appliquéd garments out by March 1; deliver the brochure design by Tuesday; bake one case of cookies by noon. Even workers with traditional jobs struggle with deadlines.

How Do You Deal with Deadlines?

1. Set hours.
2. Set priorities.
3. Know your limits.
4. Get outside help when needed.

Memorize these four steps and say them to yourself regularly because they are easy to forget—especially when deadlines are tight.

For many businesses, setting hours will be enough. When the clock says it's quitting time, close your office door and be done. Other businesses must work on a tighter schedule that requires odd or extra hours. If that's your situation, schedule the time you think the job will take when you agree to do the work.

Set priorities and don't let the business conflict with the very reasons you started your business. Don't let the pursuit of money color your vision for your family. The Bible cautions us against being purely money-motivated: "Do not weary yourself to gain wealth; cease from your consideration of it" (Proverbs 23: 4). It's easy to let the workload get out of hand, especially in a growing business. Just remember your priorities and why you wanted to work at home in the first place.

Know your limit as to how much work you can take on. There's nothing worse than taking on more work than you can handle especially if no one is available to help when you need it or if the new project or order conflicts with other commitments you have. Don't promise more than you can deliver even if you have to turn down work. Overload can be a major source of home-business stress.

When you do take on more work than you can handle, get outside assistance to help you meet your deadline. The help may just be temporary to get you through the tough spot, but if your business is growing to the point that more consistent outside aid is necessary, don't delay in getting help. It could mean the difference between business growth and business failure.

Business help can come from a number of sources. Try recruiting the kids. Hiring them will not only help you, but will teach your children a great many things as well. You could also hire an outsider. Be careful to check your zoning regulations, since they often prohibit workers who do not live at your residence from working in your home business. If that's the case and if you have the desire and the room, look into a live-in employee. It's a possibility for some.

You will, however, save yourself headaches and endless paperwork if you do not need a regular worker. Consider hiring a person as a contract worker instead of an employee.

Finally, have your spouse join you full-time in the business. The number of couples engaged in business together at home is growing. This arrangement offers numerous family advantages and the opportunity for business growth.

You can also barter help with friends or business associates and check into contract service employees or temporary help.

Problem number 5: Your work is cluttering your home. If you can't find the dining room table or walk through the bedroom because of your work paraphernalia, it's time to get organized. You need to try to separate your work physically from the areas of the home you live in.

Leaving craft supplies or computer equipment on the kitchen table means they have to be moved before dinner can be served. You and your family will quickly tire of this hassle and of seeing the mess. You will also feel like you are never away from the business if it is constantly around you. In whatever way you can, physically separate your family life from your business life.

It is important to define your workspace for your family as well as your business. If your workspace is a separate room, the boundaries are clear. When you shut the office door, you are in your work environment. If you do not have a separate room for your office, borrow space from an existing room. *Home Offices and Workspaces* also suggests hallways, staircase landings, and under-the-stairway areas as possible work areas. With proper lighting and ventilation, even a small closet can become an office. Just be sure your work area is defined. Even if you are creating an office at home where no room exists, separate that area with some sort of physical barrier.

Another way to keep your work separate from the family is to establish house rules. When you first begin your business, discuss with your family what the ground rules will be. For example, I have tried to teach my children that Mommy's closed door means she is working. What noise level will you allow? It's important to let your children know what you expect in this regard. Will you allow them to bring toys into your work area? What are the house rules when business visitors arrive? Knowing the rules in advance makes balancing your work and your family easier.

Another good way to keep your work from invading your home is to keep all your supplies, equipment, current projects, and files in one location. If you spread them out in your home, you'll tend to be more disorganized. If you keep everything together, you will be able to find things faster and easier without having to hunt for them or trek across the house when you need an item that's not at your desk. Also, your family will know to stay out of your things if all of your work is in one location. It's much easier to explain to the kids, "This area is Mommy's office; please don't touch anything in here" than it is to say "Don't touch the things in the corner, on the top of the dryer, and on the workbench in the garage."

One other inexpensive option to handling the space demands of a new business is to rent a small storage unit. These self-storage or mini-storage centers can provide real benefits for a home office by either storing the family belongings once the office has taken over the storage room at home or storing the merchandise, inventory, or noncurrent paperwork of the business. This storage area may also qualify as a business address in areas where you are not permitted to hold inventory in a private residence. (Keep in mind that you have to plan ahead to make as few trips to the warehouse as possible.)

Problem number 6: Breaks are few and far between. By living and working in the same place, you can often get the feeling that you are never away from your work. Long hours and bad habits can result. People who work for themselves often have a tendency to work harder than if they were working for someone else. If you are prone to work through lunch or dinner, force yourself to stop and take a break or eat a meal. One home-worker said, "I make myself stop and eat regularly when I'm working, even if I just stop for 20 minutes. That way I feel better and I'm more productive. Office workers take lunch hours, so we should too."

If you don't control the amount of time you spend in your business, it will begin to control you. Never forget that your family needs your time too.

Tips to Keep Home Life from Invading Work

- Be organized in your home.
- Delegate.
- Separate yourself mentally from things in your home.
- Straighten up before beginning work.
- Physically separate your work area.
- Set house rules with your family.
- Set business hours.
- Schedule time each week for your home responsibilities.
- Limit TV.
- Schedule snack/meal breaks.
- Pray for and develop discipline.

Tips to Keep Work from Invading Home Life

- Be organized in your work.

- Use voice mail, an answering machine, or a service.
- Get a business line.
- Set business hours.
- Set start/end times for meetings.
- Encourage others to drop off or pick up while you are away.
- Conduct business by mail/fax/computer whenever possible.
- Get outside help when you need it.
- Know your work limits.
- Set priorities.
- Have a separate work area.
- Keep your work materials in one location.

Some of the problems that keep you from working in your business are the same problems that keep you from enjoying your home life. That means solving a problem in one area can help what's happening in the other. Also, know that you need to make a conscious effort to protect your home life from an all-out invasion by your business life.

Managing
Your Business

W hen one writer looked at some of the top companies in the world to determine the keys to their successes, he saw that these companies had one thing in common: They were brilliant on the basics and kept things simple in a complex world. To successfully manage a home business, you would do well to follow their lead. You must manage your business—your paperwork, your money, and your time as well as your home—in the most simple, most basic, and most intelligent way possible. In this chapter we'll talk about keeping track of your paperwork and your money. To do that, begin with the basics—an organized and workable system.

Organize, Organize, Organize!

It's been said that disorganization causes 80 percent of overcrowding. Think about it—if you clean out your messy, crowded coat closet, you do two things: you throw out what you don't need and you organize what you do need. And when you're finished you usually have more room for the family coats! Author Emilie Barnes has a complete home-maintenance system built around that principle. The coat-closet principle needs to be applied to your business as well. Organize—and then toss out the unessential.

Use whatever gimmicks help you successfully organize the necessities of your business: files, business cards, addresses, phone numbers, computer disks, canceled checks, magazines, and any other paperwork your business generates. Go to a large office supply store and discover what is available (you might be surprised at the variety). Determine what you have in your office that needs organizing and then purchase or make an appropriate storage system.

Addresses, phone numbers, and business cards can be organized in Rolodex boxes or rings, address books, or card files, and, of course, on computers. With easy-to-use computer scanners, you can scan the information off a card and store the information in your database. Databases also allow you to search for your contact by key word, to code each entry for generating category-specific mailings, and to keep track of the last contact date, to name a few things. Some people also use the computer for note-taking during phone calls.

At the very least, be sure you have some type of phone message system near your phone. For archive purposes, a bound book is preferable to loose papers.

Check your computer store for different types of computer disk storage. Such systems come in flat containers, upright models, and plastic or wooden boxes. Always keep a record of your file titles, since it can be easy to forget what you named a particular document. (There are computer programs that do this for you as well.) Instead of keeping your files on your disks in chronological order, try labeling disks for each type of file that you might have, such as projects, clients, invoices, and programs.

Files can be stored in filing cabinets (cardboard, metal, or wood), old moving boxes, or even orange crates. Stationery stores carry cardboard boxes made just for storing canceled checks and back issues of magazines. Bookshelves can be anything from hand-rubbed oak to plywood and cinder blocks. The more organized you are in storing your business information, the faster and easier you can find what you need when you need it.

A Filing System

Setting up an efficient, workable, and well-organized filing system is vital to your business management. Many people recommend the basic Pendaflex system that's available in letter or legal size from most office supply and discount department stores. Larger hanging file folders hold manila folders with more specific headings.

When setting up your filing system, determine which files are most important. Which files get used the most? You need to keep those in the front of the filing cabinet. Ideally, you should be able to find everything in a minute or two. Many people prefer to alphabetize even the hanging files, but if the set of files you use most often is in the back of your file cabinet, it becomes more difficult to reach them in a hurry or when you are on the phone. Instead, alphabetize the individual manila file folders within the division file folders. Let me explain.

You can set your files up with clear, specific headings such as: Projects (particular jobs), Clients (particular people), General Business (filed by subjects, such as "Couriers," "Laser Printer"), Correspondence, Finances ("Paid Bills," "Accounts Receivable"), and Futures. You can put these headings on the file section folders, which are available in different colors for coding the different sections of your filing system.

A Futures file (sometimes called a tickler file) is used in the news business to keep track of upcoming events and stories, but it can be useful in a home business as well. Take 31 manila file folders and label each consecutively 1 to 31. As you process your mail or note an upcoming event or project, put the information in the file with the corresponding date, always keeping the current day's file in the front. Each morning check that file and put it in the back when you are through. You may want to check the next day's date in the evening to help you plan your day. If you get a flier on a seminar you want to attend on the fifteenth, put it in the folder labeled "15" in addition to marking your appointment book or calendar. This system enables you to not only keep up with your appointments and projects but also to know where the corresponding information about each thing is. You can locate that information in seconds.

Don't leave files lying around in your "file pile"; use it or lose it. When your files begin to get crowded, sort through them and remove the inactive files to a storage box. My filing system got so packed at one point (because I failed to purge the old files) that I could hardly get any of the files in or out. That inefficiency wastes time.

Record-Keeping

Keeping accurate records is very important for two simple reasons. Without them 1) you won't know if you are making or losing money and 2) you won't get all the tax deductions to which you are entitled. A good bookkeeping system is the key to your company's fiscal health—and you don't need to have an accounting background to set up and keep good books.

First, hang on to everything related to your business finances, and file those papers as soon as you get them. Believe it or not, some people have actually thrown out their bank statements because they didn't think they needed to keep them. People are often intimidated at tax time and put off preparing their taxes because they have not kept accurate records. If you keep up with your record-keeping as you go along, you will be ready and waiting when the tax man cometh. You will also be a better business manager, since keeping good records is the key to knowing how you are doing.

For some people, either the lack of know-how or the inability to see the importance of a system keeps them from having accurate records. I fell into that category when I first started my business. I am the sort of person who likes to have a calculator for any and all math functions and would rather have my teeth drilled than learn accounting. I have this crazy aversion to numbers. Therefore, when I first began my business, I had a tough row to hoe. While I was still learning what record-keeping was, my husband proceeded to set me straight. He handed me a set of papers with columns printed on them and headings like "receivables" and "expenses" and then told me to record everything for the past three months, since he couldn't make heads or tails of my records. Boy, was that fun! I thought I had my own system, but obviously it wasn't working very well.

Since my husband also happens to be my own personal accountant, he determined to teach me a little about keeping good records. With my live-in CPA, I had no choice but to get past my irrational fear of numbers and accounting lingo. Due to my nature, I will never join my husband in opening up a computer bookkeeping service, but I have learned a great deal about the importance of being organized and up-to-date in my record-keeping.

A good friend of mine started her own business from her home, and before she had been operational for even two days, she had reams of paperwork filed neatly in a notebook. I must say it took me a bit longer to learn this skill than it did for her, but the point is that if I can, anyone can.

Keeping good records doesn't mean you have to drown in paper. There are several convenient systems for transferring paperwork to computer storage. By scanning in correspondence, invoices, and customer information, you can transform the amount of paper that would fill two filing cabinets onto a small disk. Scanners can convert both typed words into data using OCR (Optical Character Recognition) programs and artwork (which take up more computer space) into graphics files. These new computer documents can be organized using computer storage devices and tape back-up systems. These systems are real space savers for someone whose office is limited to a small room in the home. With careful organization and data management, you can easily retrieve information. Some systems even automatically index every word of every file for easy searching, and with some you can even choose your own indexing key words.

A Record-Keeping System

Most home-business owners keep their accounting system simple. They do it themselves—and not necessarily on the computer. A variety of simple bookkeeping systems can be purchased at your local office supply store. For those who already own computers, many accounting packages are available at modest prices to make keeping records and compiling monthly reports as easy as possible.

To keep track of all of your expenses and income and to be sure you get it all recorded in your books, consider this easy-to-use system. Label two large envelopes Business Income and Business Expenses. Put them somewhere in your work area where they are easily accessible. Try taping them up near your desk or tacking them to the wall or on a bulletin board. These envelopes will help you keep track of all transactions that fall into two categories.

Business Income: In this envelope keep copies of all checks, receipts of all sales, or bank deposit slips that list the name or number of the check. Simply put, keep a record of all business income.

Business Expenses: In this envelope keep receipts (even hand-written ones) for every penny you spend on your business—stubs from paid business bills or canceled checks that you wrote for business expenses.

At the end of the month, tally all the records in each envelope to see how much you spent and how much you received as income. Staple together each month's records and keep them in their respective envelopes, so that determining the quarterly or year-to-date figures will be simple. Whether your record-keeping system is done by hand or is computerized, keep it up-to-date. If you fall behind entering your records into your bookkeeping system, it is simple to catch up. You don't have to scrounge around trying to find invoices here and receipts there to make your journal entries. This system makes it easy to keep your income and expense information organized and your business records up-to-date. If properly used, this method becomes a habit.[1]

Finally, always separate your business and personal finances. By doing this you will be able to more easily see each month where your business stands financially, budgeting will be simpler, and tax time will be easier because your records will be clearer.

Keeping Track of Expenses

It's easy to lose track of expenses if you lose track of your receipts. Many home-business owners begin spending money for the business before they have a business account. A business expense is easier to lose track of that way, and since most such expenses are tax-deductible, you won't want to miss a single one. One simple way to be sure you keep all records is to carry one of your business envelopes in your purse or wallet. When you are out and find that you have made a purchase that is business-related, put the receipt in that envelope at the time of the purchase. When you get home, put it in the appropriate larger envelope.

Another thing you won't want to neglect is business use of your auto. You will want to keep an accurate record of the miles you put on the family car while you are out and about for business purposes. This may be automatic for you, but I had a tough time remembering at first. It seemed like I was always in a hurry and never remembered to write down my mileage or car expenses when I got home. Sometimes I would write the number down on a gas ticket, grocery bag, or whatever else was handy, but this kind of record-keeping resulted in a real hodgepodge. Often I thought I had recorded everything, but when I looked at my record at the end of the month, I knew I had driven more business miles than I had recorded. So I bought a little 49-cent spiral notebook (or you can purchase an auto mileage book) and a small pen which I inserted in the spiral binding. I attached it to my sun visor and made it a habit to never get out of the car without writing down the mileage right then. I developed another habit: Before I get out of the car, I zero out my trip odometer. Then when I get into the car I don't have to think about the number of miles on the odometer, nor do I have to subtract from the mileage when I finish driving. I only have to think about my mileage once—right before I get out of the car when I get home. I look at the trip odometer, record it in my spiral book, zero out the counter so I'm ready for my next trip, and I'm done. It takes only seconds each time, but it's a good system and I'm always up-to-date.

All kinds of books and resources offer the small business owner specific how-tos of good record-keeping. More important than the type of system you have is the fact that you have a system at all.

One last word. Some people say that if you spend over half an hour a day on business finances, it is time to get help. Depending on the size of your business and your needs, you can hire a part-time bookkeeper or an accountant, or you can computerize your accounting system.

Better Business Management

- **Know where you stand each month**—Balance your account. Know your true balance at all times. Check your envelopes and sort them.

- **Know your expenses**—Where is all of your money going each month?

- **Know what bills you owe**—Record them daily as they come in. Know when they are due.

- **Know where all your records are**—Make it a habit to file receipts, work orders, client files, and payment information as soon as they come in—and be able to find whichever of these you need within three minutes.

- **Know where everything is**—Make sure your filing system is well-organized.

- **Know the time you have invested**—Know at the end of each day how you used your time. You will know if you are being productive. If you aren't productive, you can work to improve. You must also know your time if you bill clients or customers accordingly.

- **Know your inventory**—Check your inventory daily. What products do you have on hand? What supplies?

Know what you've sold and, if necessary, the amount of sales tax you've collected. Keep a log and control your inventory. Don't let your supplies run too low, so you won't be caught unable to fill an order or do a job. I once got a large volume of laser printing for a client. About halfway through the printing, my toner cartridge ran out. To give the client his work when I had promised, I had to purchase a new cartridge at more than double what I normally pay. (It takes several days to get them at my lower rate.) By not keeping track of the condition of my supplies, I got low on a business commodity and had to pay for my oversight.

- **Know your invoicing status**—Invoice clients daily or weekly, depending on your business. I invoice as I finish a job. That way I never have to wonder if I did it. If invoicing is done in a timely fashion, you won't miss out on money owed to you because of sloppy record-keeping.

About Your Money

Don't plan on making a profit for the first few months. In fact, most traditional businesses expect to operate in the red for the first couple of years. However, because you are operating your business from your home with little overhead, you should normally see a profit before that long a time. By carefully managing your money and periodically evaluating your financial condition, you will see a profit as quickly as possible.

Small-business (and home-based) financial consultant Vera Peirsol of Vapco Services, Inc., recommends doing a profit-and-loss statement at the end of every month or at least at the end of each quarter. These statements help you compare how you are doing with your budget. Comparing what you have made with what you have spent each month will also give you a clear understanding of how healthy your business is.

Furthermore, looking at these financial reports will help you prepare financial projections. After the first three months, take a good long look at your balance sheet. Compare your profit-and-loss statement and expenditures with your budget. Determine if you need to be spending more or less in any area. Do you need to add a business phone line, buy more equipment, hire some additional help, reduce inventory or supplies, or produce more or less advertising? As you evaluate these things, estimate how much you think you will grow in the coming months. When you forecast your financial growth, you are creating a target. Without a business target to shoot for, you will stay where you are or be ill-prepared to handle growth.

To realize a profit as soon as possible in your business and to continue to be prosperous, remember two important rules. First, don't spend money you haven't earned and, second, control your costs. It's so easy to get into debt and so difficult to get out! In some situations business debt might be advised, but don't get yourself in any more of a financial bind than necessary. One person I interviewed explained how she kept costs down and learned to trust God for her business at the same time: "I didn't hire a delivery service. I got a pizza delivery guy to make my deliveries in his spare time at a fraction of the cost. I didn't get slick, glossy, beautiful labels for my products printed right off the bat, but instead used mailing labels. You have to be really humble. I intend to have a refrigerated delivery truck, my own bakery, and the slick, glossy labels in the future, but people often put out a lot of money and then they're bound to their businesses. For me, the Lord can't work as well then because it's harder to listen with creditors at my door. On the other hand, I have to be willing to let go of dollars when necessary. It's a matter of balance."

Are You Managing Your Money Properly?

You will be if you remember these points:

- Know your bank balance.
- Pay your bills on time.

- Invoice each week.

- Control your costs.

- Try to earn money before you spend it.

- Know where your money is going.

Cash Flow

Simply defined, cash flow is cash receipts less cash expenses for any given period. Hopefully you'll get that check that's "in the mail" before your bills come due! To have a healthy cash flow, you must continue to generate new business and collect on that business as soon as you can. That's the bottom line. To help alleviate cash-flow problems, consider the following points:

- Aim for COD (cash on delivery) for services or products whenever possible.

- When you take on new business (particularly if you are a service business), get a percentage down in advance, thereby providing you with operating capital.

- Bill out at least every 30 days.

- Offer a discount to your customers if they pay your invoice within ten days of the date of the statement. One home-business owner who did this said, "Eighty percent of my billings are in by the tenth or fifteenth of the month since I began to offer the discount. I usually have a 100-percent collection rate every month. If I don't, the client knows I don't work for him the next month until I get paid."

- Have "Payment Due Upon Receipt" printed on every invoice.

- Get credit from your suppliers. If you can get a 10-, 30-, or even 60-day net with some suppliers, you will do a lot toward minimizing cash-flow difficulties.

- Prioritize your bills. Know which bills are the most important. First pay the debts that are collateralized. If you don't make your house payment, they can take your house. Next pay your utilities. If you don't have electricity or a phone, you can't run your business. Third, pay your suppliers. If you don't have a good relationship with them and keep supplies on hand, doing business will be very difficult.

- Deal with your creditors honestly. Never say the check is in the mail if it isn't. If you plan on paying a business bill after a certain check comes in and that client doesn't pay you on time, call your creditor and tell him or her the situation. Instead of this forthrightness hurting your credibility, he or she will probably respect you for being honest. We are subject to a higher authority anyway, so operating honestly should be second nature to Christian business people.

- Project your cash flow between the first and the fifteenth and identify which of your bills will come due during that time. Do the same for the remainder of the month. If you don't have enough billed out to meet that month's obligations, let your creditors know this and ask them for an extension. Or get your suppliers to give you terms for 60 days. If the imbalance continues, you need to get serious about increasing your monthly billings. Generate more cash! Market, market, market for new business.

To Ensure That You Are Paid

Try to protect yourself in advance against collection difficulties by using a financial agreement, preferably written rather than verbal. Such an agreement is basically a contract of terms and is highly recommended, especially in service businesses. Have one basic agreement for which you can fill in the blanks for each client. Include:

1. The details of the job.

2. Payment arrangements.

3. Hourly rate or base price.

4. Special terms (such as 50 percent down, 50 percent upon completion).

5. Start and completion dates.

6. Signatures of you and your client.

Have your customer sign the agreement and give him a copy, keeping one for yourself.

What to Do If Clients Won't Pay

Invoice them again with "Past Due" printed in boldface on the bill. If they still don't pay within ten days, call and ask when you can expect payment. If they are having difficulties or owe on a current and past invoice, arrange a payment plan with them to assure them that you are willing to negotiate. If you show that you are willing to work with them, they will be more likely to pay you. If you suspect, however, that your client is a deadbeat, get tough! You don't need that kind of client in the first place.

A friend of mine is a soft-spoken, mild-mannered woman—and she is excellent at collections. Once a company gave her trouble about paying her invoice. After gentle reminders, she visited their office and threatened to drive up and down the street with a sign on her car proclaiming, "X Company owes me $2,000 and won't pay!" Needless to say, she left that day with her check. Several weeks later the company folded, but she got her money!

Another tactic is to call and ask when your check will be ready and tell them you will be by in person to pick it up. If they say it's not ready when you get there, tell them you'll wait!

Collection agencies and small claims court are a last resort.

Bartering

Check your phone directory for bartering clubs in your area. They can save you money and provide goods or services that you might not otherwise be able to afford. Even if you don't join a club, you might be surprised by the number of people who are open to bartering services. I designed an advertising flier for a company in exchange for their referral service and we both saved money. The IRS has specific rules about bartering in terms of taxable income and deductible expenses, so be sure to check with your accountant first. Keep records of any bartering in which you engage.

One woman in Massachusetts who runs a home-based word-processing business depleted her resources in the beginning with a $20,000 investment in home office equipment. Many people don't have that kind of funding and would never be able to start home businesses without some creative ways to come up with the needed resources and equipment. In some instances bartering can be the solution.

Another home-worker bartered her typesetting services in exchange for the equipment she needed. "I was fortunate. I was able to purchase my equipment because a client financed it in exchange for work I did for her. That led to other word-of-mouth jobs." The client was happy because she received a needed service. The home-worker was thrilled since it gave her the means to start her own business with very little capital.

Bartering is exactly how I started my own business. I was the managing editor of a trade publication, and I designed and typeset the magazine on my employer's computer. I wanted a computer of my own, so my employer financed one for me. We just deducted the monthly cost of the computer from the income I received for editing and laying out the magazine. In a short time I owned my own equipment, which enabled me to take on other jobs and eventually start my own business from my home. By using a type of barter arrangement, I was able to start small, without depleting my resources or getting a loan. The company provided what I needed, and I provided a service for them.

Tips for Good Business Organization

- Write your business plan.
- Have organized files.
- Have a good record-keeping system and use it diligently.
- Evaluate your monthly expenses against your business budget.
- Maintain your cash flow. Keep tabs on your monthly income compared to your business bills.
- Evaluate your financial reports monthly.
- Forecast financial growth.

Managing your own business need not be as intimidating as some people think. Organize your business information, keep accurate records, and stay on top of your finances. If you do those three things, you will be on your way to a prosperous and well-managed home business. But don't stop there; remember to take your business problems to the Lord. He cares very much about the details in our lives and earnestly desires to lead us. We should strive to become excellent business managers as we seek direction and wisdom from the Lord.

"The mind of man plans his way, but the Lord directs his steps" (Proverbs 16: 9).

Managing
Your Time

Why is it that some people climb mountains while others struggle with molehills? One of the biggest reasons is *time management*. People who get a lot done use each hour to their advantage. They are thrifty with their time: They carefully consider how they spend it. Those who are left in the dust midway up their molehills usually don't evaluate whether they are using their time effectively. Many people simply do not know how to manage their day.

Home-business owner Stacy described her surprise at the difficulty of managing her time: "It's harder to get things done than I ever thought it would be. It takes more phone calls, more looking for things, and just more time to get things accomplished." When Mike was asked what he wished he had known when he first started his business, his response was "Just how much time running a business from home really takes. I had to learn through trial and error how much time everything takes. I needed to do some preplanning to figure out how to make it all work for me. I wish I had worked out a time-management strategy before I jumped into it."

Since the timing of almost everything you do in your day builds on the activity just preceding it, you get a kind of snowball effect. If you wake up late and have a full day planned, you're off to a bad start. If you have to pick up the cleaning by 5, but your 4 o'clock meeting ran too long, you had better plan to wear something else tomorrow. Furthermore, things usually take twice as long as you think they will. With interruptions, a two-hour job can easily turn into four hours. To learn to better gauge how much time things will really take, make a list of all your projects or activities and estimate how long you think each will take. Then at the end of the day write down how long each task actually took. Chances are that you probably underestimated.[1] Learning to properly estimate the time needed to complete your tasks is one of the most vital keys to effectively using your time.

If your time management skills could use some sharpening, you're not alone. Time management has become big business. All kinds of systems—from "daytimers" to CDs, from workshops to workbooks—are available to help us manage our time effectively. For the home-business person, managing how you spend your day is critical. You need to get mileage out of your minutes! How can you do that? Be organized. Be flexible. Schedule your time. Don't procrastinate. And dedicate each day to the Lord.

Be Organized

An organized approach to time management is just as important as an organized approach to business management.

1. *Use a System*

Many people are good list-makers, writing down what they must do each day, but with a home business demanding your time and attention, a more detailed organizational system could serve you well. Instead of having various notes or lists lying around the house, try using an organizer. There are many different types available from office supply stores and department stores. You can even make your own with a three-ring binder and notebook paper. The basics include the following categories: a yearly, monthly, and weekly calendar; things to do today; and an address/phone number list. You might also want to include a section for current and long-range goals. You can personalize your organizer for your lifestyle, preferences, and particular home business. Then you'll have, in one spot, your list of what to do today, tomorrow, next week, and next month. Combining your "to-do list" with your appointment diary, calendar, and address book can save you much time.

Time-management software integrates calendars, daily activities, appointments (with alarm features), contact information, and more. You might also look into the many electronic personal communicator systems known by names such as "personal digital assistants" (PDAs), like the Palm Pilot. PDAs combine scheduling and calendar capabilities with electronic note taking, paging, and even e-mail. Most are equipped to "synch" with computers. A variety of versions are available from many different companies. No matter what type of gadget you prefer to keep you organized and on time, use one to your advantage.

2. Set Goals

If you want to accomplish something, set a goal. Some studies have shown that people who write down their goals are 90 times more likely to accomplish them than those who don't. So write down your daily, weekly, monthly, and yearly goals. Be specific about what you want to accomplish in each given time period. You can even go a step further: Write down your medium-range and long-range goals as well. But don't stop there. Also write down the steps you need to take to make your goals a reality—a road map, if you will, to your destination.

If your daily goal is to get one new client, your action plan might be "Call five new prospects." If your daily goal is to finish your current project, your action plan would be to type ten pages, or bake seven dozen muffins, or take whatever specific steps are necessary to accomplish that goal. This goal-setting action-plan idea works for long-range goals as well as for small daily tasks. If you want to build a country home, start a second business, or go into business with your spouse, write down what you need to do in order to accomplish that goal. Include a timetable for getting it done. After all, goals are just dreams with deadlines.[2]

3. *Prioritize Your Activities*

After writing down what you must do, the next step is to determine the order of importance of the things on that list. What absolutely must be done before the day is over? What would you like to have done? What can wait until tomorrow? Give the items on your list a 1, 2, 3-type rating and tackle them accordingly. If you get to the end of the list, great! If you get to the end of the day first, move the objectives you didn't accomplish to the top of your list for tomorrow.

Be Flexible

When considering how to manage your time, one of the most sanity-saving tidbits to remember is *be flexible!* Working where you live mandates a certain level of flexibility. Children, telephones, doorbells, housework, and neighbors can make it nearly impossible to get things done at times. If you had planned on working at your desk from 2 to 5 o'clock, but at 2:45 your washing machine overflows, you have to shift your plans. If you were to work at an "outside" job, you wouldn't even have known about the problem until you walked in the door at the end of the day. But when you're at home you can't just slosh through the mess. You stop what you're doing, clean it up, and finish your work another time.

And don't forget to be flexible for the fun things as well. Occasionally you may have your day planned, but a friend will call and say, "My uncle loaned me his catamaran today. Do you want to go for an afternoon sail?" A steady diet of abandoning scheduled work for a day of fun can lead to an unhealthy business, but being flexible enough to occasionally enjoy a spur-of-the-moment activity is one of the reasons people work from their homes.

Schedule Your Time

1. *Schedule Time for Paperwork.*

Set aside a certain time each day or week to do your paperwork. File your receipts. Invoice your clients. Balance your account. Pay your bills. Don't wait until the bank is calling, your creditors are knocking, and your in-box is overflowing. Depending on the size and nature of your business, schedule time daily or weekly to tend to your paperwork. Put it on your calendar.

2. *Don't Fragment Your Time.*

One way to make the most of your time is to divide your day into similar activities by category. Organize your business tasks with your household tasks. Since you work at home, you don't need to keep business and personal activities separated during your day. You don't have to wait until 5 o'clock to stop for milk. You can do it on the way to the office supply store or along with other business errands.

Plan to do your phone-calling in the morning. It's easier to catch people then. Also, plan your errands during non-rush hour (another home-working perk). Group your errands by proximity. Think through what you need to do before you leave home. Order your errands along the shortest route, not just by what must be done first.

Shifting to and from various modes throughout the day wastes time and is unproductive. So, as you group similar things together, try to finish doing one kind of activity before you shift to another.

I may be in the mommy mode, wife mode, business professional mode, and homemaker mode throughout a given day, but I try to group similar activities from these different modes together. By grouping my activities, I save start-and-stop time, and my leisure time comes in larger segments as well. I find it much more enjoyable to finish all my work and then have undisturbed time with my family.

3. *Work at the Time That Is Most Productive.*

Determine when you are most productive. When do you have the most energy? When do you think most clearly? What time of day do you most like to work? When do you get sleepy or sluggish? Evaluate these factors in light of your family's schedule. Strive to work during your peak performance period if that does not conflict too much with the routine of your family.

4. *Establish Some Type of Routine.*

You don't have to be limited to the nine-to-five routine (or the "Sesame Street" to "Mr. Rogers' Neighborhood" schedule!). Whether you have come from the corporate world or the "kiddie corner," set up some type of routine that works for you. Even people who hate routine can benefit from some semblance thereof. If you plan a time to work, you will accomplish more in that given period than if you just work when you are so moved.

Some people are most efficient with their time when they log the traditional nine-to-five hours in their home office. Others like to work in their businesses part of the day and in their homes the other part. Still others work in the business only on certain days and take several days off during the week. Many businesses tend to be seasonal, with longer hours required during, for example, holidays or tax time.

If you like a lot of structure in your life and don't have children, you may want to stick to traditional office hours. If you have school-age children, try to get the bulk of your work done before three o'clock in the afternoon. If you hate routine, working at home gives you the option of working hard for several days and then taking some time off. Whatever routine you choose, and however rigid you make it, is entirely up to you. Even just establishing as a goal for yourself "I will try to work at home _____" (you fill in the blank as to when) will lead to a more effective use of your time.

5. *Be Selective About What You Take On.*

Before you say yes to a friend, a project, or a job, consider how that decision will affect you in the coming hours, days, or weeks. Do you have enough time to fulfill your obligation without having it complicate other things in your schedule? It's easy to say yes too readily and then realize after we're in the middle of things that we haven't planned our time properly to meet obligations. So before you say yes to something, be sure you look carefully at how that something will affect you, your family, and your other commitments.

6. *Work Backward When Scheduling Your Activities.*

First list all the things you want to accomplish and then note the amount of time you think it will take you to accomplish each thing. Count backward from the time you need to be done. If you have a project that is due by next week, figure out how many days you have left to accomplish your task. Divide the steps necessary to meet that goal into daily assignments until your project is complete or your deadline has been met. Don't just work on a project without paying attention to your time frame. Whether it's a month-long project or an hour-long task, know where you need to be at any given point.

7. *Schedule Extra Time.*

When making your schedule, give yourself some padding in your appointments and activities. Build in extra time for those occasions when you get lost, the baby spits up on you as you are walking out the door, or you get into the car and find that the gas gauge is on empty. If you have some padding in your time schedule, you can deal with these minor inconveniences without having them become major dilemmas. Don't book your schedule too tightly. If you schedule an extra 15 minutes between appointments and nothing goes wrong, you will be early. That's much better than having no time cushion, encountering a problem, and arriving late and frazzled.

8. *When Scheduling Meetings, Evaluate Their Importance.*

Is this meeting really necessary? Many meetings waste time because you could just as easily accomplish the same thing by e-mail, phone or fax. So don't hesitate to set the length of a meeting in advance or to assertively and tactfully end a meeting that is dragging. Unproductive meetings are big time robbers.

Some unproductive meetings you won't mind—if you are with people you want to be with and you have the time. In fact, meetings like that are one way to avoid the isolation that some home-workers feel. However, if you would rather spend your time with someone else or if time is short, decide whether you must actually meet in person to do what needs to be done.

9. *Ask How You Should Spend Your Time.*

Some experts say that you should spend 50 percent of your time making your product or providing your service, 25 percent of your time marketing your business, and 25 percent of your time running your business.[3] Other sources say that entrepreneurs actually spend their business time in keeping records, direct selling, production, maintenance, dealing with suppliers, arranging financial matters, planning, and dealing with employees.

It's common for people who start a small business to do so during the years that they start their families, often working long hours when the businesses as well as the children are young. So be thoughtful in the amount of time you allot to each.

Just as you should carefully consider how to spend your time, also consider how not to spend your time. Are you spending time on things that are not productive or that do not contribute to your personal, family, or spiritual life? First let's consider television. It's a simple fact—people who watch a lot of TV cannot accomplish what they could if they limited their viewing. Television has been accused of being the great national babysitter, the roadblock to literacy, a force undermining the family, and one of the greatest time-wasters known to man. TV desensitizes us, stifles our creativity, thwarts our imagination, robs us of personal communication, and negatively influences us in a number of ways. Some people are opting to pitch the set entirely! One family described what happened when they drastically limited the amount of television in their home:

"After three months my wife and I began to see things happen. Suddenly we had the time each night as a family to read aloud, to read to ourselves, to do homework at an unhurried pace, to learn how to play chess and checkers...to draw and paint and color, and—best of all—to talk with each other, asking questions and answering questions. Our children's imaginations were coming back to life again."[4]

Furthermore, it's hard to hear that still, small voice of God when the TV is blaring. One author, a simple country preacher, said that he felt God guiding him to give up the two hours of TV he watched at night after the kids were in bed. Instead, he spent that time in prayer. Shortly after making that decision, and during that time with the Lord, he felt God guiding him in some specific ways. That night played an important part in the ministry of David Wilkerson, founder of Teen Challenge.

Even though there were some good entertaining and educational programs on television and my children were familiar with Bert and Ernie, at times I wished the TV would blow up. When you have a home business, time is very limited. We need to learn to control the monster in our living rooms instead of allowing it to control us.

Tips to Controlling Your Television

- Move it out of the living room.
- Don't let it be the focal point of the room.
- Put it in a cabinet with doors.
- Keep it unplugged.
- Determine a time limit for your own viewing and your children's.

• Keep alternative entertainment sources handy, making it easy to grab something besides the "on" switch.

10. *Get your family's cooperation.*

If you have decided that you would like to work according to a certain schedule, make sure your family knows when you will be working and when you won't be. Set ground rules and enlist their help.

Don't Procrastinate

Procrastination is probably the biggest reason why people fail to accomplish their goals and meet their deadlines. After all, when we procrastinate, we get lazy. We lose momentum. We miss out on opportunities. We are late. We get ourselves in a time crunch. We forfeit peace in our lives and generally get ourselves in a tizzy.

I know all about this from firsthand experience because I am a "recovering procrastinator." There were those high-school days when I would rush in at 9 o'clock at night and say, "Daddy, you just have to type this history paper for me. It's due in the morning, and my grade depends on it!" There were those Christmases when I waited until the last minute to shop and then had to settle for hot pink wool socks for my grandmother.

I'm not talking about situations where you genuinely take on more than you can handle and, as a result, get swamped. Nor am I talking about extenuating circumstances that arise and throw a kink in your otherwise-well-laid-out plans. I'm talking about pure and simple procrastination—putting off what you know you need to be doing. There will be plenty of situations like the first two I mentioned, but dealing with procrastination in your life can prevent many other problems.

If you are a chronic procrastinator, you can overcome this obstacle to peace and success. A slogan from a popular commercial for athletic shoes told us how: "Just do it." Don't think about it; do it. Don't overplan for it; do it. Don't just dream about it; do it. Proverbs

14:23 says, "In all labor there is profit, but mere talk leads only to poverty." Don't just talk about it. Do it.

If you are trying to finish a project or reach a goal, try this: 1) Write down your goal and the action steps you need to take to achieve it. 2) On your calendar schedule a start date, intermittent checkpoints, and a target date for completing whatever it is that you want to do. 3) Check your calendar daily so you can watch your progress. 4) Pray that the Lord will help you overcome your tendency to put things off. If laziness is the reason you put things off, you will have difficulty making your home business a success. At the very least, you will experience frustration. As Proverbs 19:15 says, "Laziness casts into a deep sleep, and an idle man will suffer hunger." 5) Sometimes it helps to put notes around the house to remind you to begin a project. 6) Do the worst things first. Getting the most unpleasant part out of the way in the beginning can make it easier to finish. 7) Tell your spouse and family or friends that you are working on gaining control over procrastination and ask for their support and encouragement. Ask them to remind you when they notice you procrastinating and to encourage you when you succeed.

Sometimes people are good at beginning things but poor at completing them. The Bible admonishes us to finish what we start: "But now finish doing it also; that just as there was the readiness to desire it, so there may be also the completion of it by your ability" (2 Corinthians 8:11).

Dedicate Each Day to the Lord

The time you have available each day is given to you by the Lord: "There is an appointed time for everything, and there is a time for every event under heaven" (Ecclesiastes 3:1). Begin your day by dedicating it to the Lord. Ask Him for guidance and for help in using the time He has given you as He sees fit. Follow David's example. He wrote, "In the morning, O Lord, Thou wilt hear my voice; in the morning I will order my prayer to Thee and eagerly watch" (Psalm 5:3). We are accountable to the Lord for how we use our time. Therefore we should make quality use of our time.

"Quality use," however, doesn't mean being busy at every moment with some pressure-filled activity. Rest and times of inactivity are very important. Nor does quality use of time mean that our to-do list must always be finished. We should be open to God's interruptions and be ready for whatever God has planned for our day. If things are not going as planned, don't panic. God will bless your day anyway.

We are responsible for what we do with our time today, not tomorrow. Proverbs 27:1 says, "Do not boast about tomorrow, for you do not know what a day may bring forth" and Jesus Himself said, "Do not be anxious for tomorrow" (Matthew 6:34). Pray that God will guide you as you strive to use your time to make a difference in things that have eternal value.

Time-Management Tips

- **Limit outside activities**—Your time is precious. Make sure you spend your time on the important things.

- **Schedule in family time**—Plan for time to be with your spouse or children. If you and I don't do this, it's too easy to let the people closest to us get what's left over of our time and energy (if there is any left over) instead of our prime time.

- **Plan when you will spend time with the Lord**—Through prayer and Bible reading, nurture your relationship with your Creator. You need His direction, guidance, and strength to be able to handle the load you have taken on.

- **Plan some free time for yourself**—Don't leave yourself off the list. You need some R & R time as well.

- **Multitask: Learn to do more than one thing at a time**—
Talk on the phone while you prepare dinner. While you
wait in line, make a list of what you must do tomorrow.
Just be sure not to constantly multitask. Too much is
stressful and peace-robbing.

- **Learn to do things faster**—Train yourself to make snap
decisions over things that really don't matter. Save your
time and energy for the important things. Don't dawdle
over which kind of pizza to order. Just decide. Don't
make a major production over simple things in life.
Plenty of difficult situations call for more than enough of
our time, attention, and energy.

- **Use technology to save precious time**—Take full advantage of time-saving tools like high-speed ovens and such.
My food processor saves me about eight minutes each
time I use it. I use it at least three times a week, so that's
almost half an hour a week that I save. I can read a magazine, take a walk, or bake a cake in the time saved.

- **Take full advantage of electronic devices**—Use a small
voice recorder to dictate ideas as you drive, record notes
from meetings, brainstorm while you're doing laundry, or
cite reminders to yourself about projects. Cookbook
author Jill Bond keeps one on her counter as she creates
new recipes. It is so much easier to use a voice-activated
recorder than trying to jot down "Then add 3 cups of…"
on a piece of paper when her hands are wrist high in
dough.

- **Organize your files to save you time**—Many types of
businesses use "project files," but you don't even need to
have a business to benefit from organizing files according
to various projects. To save time, write the names,
numbers, addresses, and deadlines (as applicable) on

the outside of the folder. Then, when you use the material in the folder, you don't have to look elsewhere for that information when you need it—it's all right there in front of you.

- **Let your fingers do the walking**—Use your phone book before you make unnecessary trips. Calling ahead can save you not only time and money but frustration as well. Keep a phone edirectory in your car for cell phone use.

- **Keep a pen handy**—Keep a pen and paper by your bed, in your car, and in your briefcase or purse at all times. You never know when the inspiration will hit! There have been many times when I have solved a problem or come up with a great idea while trying to go to sleep. That's also the time when I occasionally remember something to do the next day that I hadn't written on my list. If you don't write it down when you think of it, you may lose the thought.

- **Take breaks**—Even a short break can give you the necessary mental and physical renewal you need to get going again.

- **Work smarter, not harder**—Use mind over muscle to save you time. Think things through to see if there is any way you can save time.

- **Don't drive during rush hour.**

- **Put idle time to work for you**—Use in-between time to your advantage. Carry with you a book or article you want to read—and read it while you stand in line. Make out your grocery list while you wait at the dentist. Empty the trash during the commercials of a program you are watching or listening to. Countless things can be done during the small snatches of time between the major activities of your day.

• **Strive to simplify your life**—The more you simplify your life, the easier it will be to manage your time.

You'll inevitably have days when your time-management system just doesn't work and you feel like you're about to lose it. When time problems get the best of you and the home business path gets a little rocky, don't stop at just counting to ten or taking a hot bubble bath. Try these five-minute breaks:

1. Quote a Scripture ("I can do all things through [Christ] who strengthens me" [Philippians 4:13]; "Do your work heartily as for the Lord" [Colossians 3:23]; "Greater is He who is in you than he who is in the world" [1 John 4:4]).

2. Pray.

3. Make a mental note of a blessing you received from the Lord that day.

4. Tell someone about that blessing. Be a testimony!

5. Hug your spouse.

6. Hug your kids.

7. Listen to Christian music.

8. Sing a praise song.

9. Read a psalm.

10. Think of three reasons why you feel the Lord has blessed you with a home business.

Managing
Your Home

To some it may sound like Utopia—running your own business from the comfort of your own home with your spouse and/or little darlings all around you. But the little darlings are not always little angels, and family life and business paraphernalia do not exactly produce tidy homes. The supermom (or superdad) syndrome is much easier to fall into when you're working at home. In fact it takes real effort to avoid trying to become one—and to avoid feeling guilty because you can't.

But don't worry—the ideal of the superperson is passé. I think women in particular are tired of feeling as if they have to reach for the brass ring and "be all that they can be" while simultaneously looking great, feeling great, and running a great home. Add a home business to that picture and you're sure to come up with an unwieldy situation. If you have ever struggled with trying to keep it all together, you are in the company of millions of others. Take solace in the fact that you actually can have it all; you just can't have it all at the same time.

The most obvious question right now is "How can I manage a business at home when managing my children and my household took all my time before?" How do you continue to have a well-managed home and also a home business? Know that you cannot do everything yourself! Reevaluate how you run your home, decide what can be eliminated, get extra help, set aside time to maintain your home, readjust your standards, and organize your home.

Reevaluate How You Run Your Home

Begin by finding a quiet place. Then seek the Lord and ask Him to give you wisdom and guidance as you plan. Next write down every single thing you do during the course of a week and when you do it. Write down anything additional that comes up during a typical month that requires your time. Note how those are divided into daily activities. You may be amazed that you have any energy left over after looking at your list! Next, on a separate piece of paper write down what you consider priorities in your life—things like your quiet time with the Lord, time alone with your husband, time to play with your kids, time for exercise, and so forth. Now go back to your activity list and put a checkmark in the margin next to all the activities that are also on your priority list. The more checkmarks you have, the better you are doing at balancing your life and doing what is important. If you don't have as many checks as you'd like, don't worry. You are now taking action to spend time on the things you value as priorities.

Decide What Can Be Eliminated

Take a good long look at your activity list and mark through anything you can cut out. At first glance you might think that nothing can be crossed off, but the more you consider your list, the more you may find that you can eliminate some of your activities. If you try to run your home as you did before and if you try to accomplish everything on your list in addition to running your business, you will run yourself into an early grave. Remember, don't try to be a superwoman. You may love that community-college class, a hobby, that Bible study, or a club you belong to, but something has to give. You may have time for these activities later in your life. If you're combining your home business with being the primary manager of your household and especially if children are in the picture, you may need to put some of the things in your life on hold. The point is to simplify your life as much as possible so that you don't go crazy trying to run your home and your home business.

Get Extra Help

And now to the fun part of the list process: Give some of your work to others! When I asked a friend how he managed everything in his life, Larry said he did three things: "Delegate. Delegate. Delegate." A good rule of thumb!

Mark all the things on the list that you can delegate. You don't have to do all the laundry. You don't have to cook all the meals all the time. Someone else can take out the garbage, and so forth. You may find you need help in your business, in your home, or with your children.

You can have your children do some of the tasks, and your husband can become your helpmate in the truest sense of the word. Having a home business will mean teamwork, so be frank in the beginning and go over the list with your family, letting them decide which things they would like to do. Some people have even had their spouses join them full-time in their home business, a move that really lightens the load.

Since one of the goals of having a business is to provide an income, use some of that income to hire someone to help you. Consider it a necessary expense for your business—not to mention your health and sanity. Dr. James Dobson has said that the fatigue-and-time-pressure syndrome is one of the top causes of depression among women. Many families have prioritized things they would like when they have enough money, but Dr. Dobson says, "It is my conviction that domestic help for the mother of small children should appear on that priority list too. Without it, she is sentenced to the same responsibilities day in and day out, seven days a week. It is my belief that she will do a more efficient job in those tasks and be a better mother if she can share the load with someone else occasionally."[1] That is especially true of the woman who is a homemaker and has a home business. You essentially have two jobs, and you will function better in both jobs if you do not bear the workload alone.

You do not have to pay for an expensive maid service if you need help cleaning the house. Teenagers or college students are often more than willing to earn some money by helping you out. A friend of mine hires a teenager in her neighborhood to do a varied assortment of odd jobs at her home, such as cleaning, ironing, cooking a meal once or twice a week, and anything she can think of to free up more of her time for the things which she cannot delegate. Another friend makes good use of the teenage babysitters she hires in the evenings, who would otherwise be watching TV after the kids are in bed. When she hires them, she asks if they want to make more than the normal hourly rate. If they say yes, she leaves a list of simple things to do.

To find help with your cleaning, put a note on the bulletin board at your church describing the kind of help you need. Call other area churches and ask if they know of people looking for work. Run an ad in your community paper. Tell your friends that you want to hire some help. Call a local high school counselor and ask for the names of responsible students. Or you can use a maid service. That is usually pretty expensive, but it might be worth it if you just need occasional help and you don't have any other means of getting it. As Luanne Shackelford has said, "It's cheaper than room and board in the funny farm."[2]

Some of my clients and friends used to accuse me of being supermom as I tried to run my business, keep my children at home, home-school, freelance in the news reporting business, write, and so on. I am not this all-together wonder-woman. I simply have outside help, and I don't do all of those things at the same time. In the beginning I tried to do everything myself. Things would go okay for awhile, but then the work would begin to accumulate, as would the laundry and the dishes. Sometimes it looked like World War III had broken out in our house. I knew I would probably have more time with my children, my husband, and my house if I just got a "normal" job, but I was committed to working at home. One day was particularly bad. It was 1:00 in the morning, and I was working on a deadline. My kids had vegged out in front of the TV, toys were everywhere, no one had clean clothes, the bathrooms were a mess, and we had ordered dinner out (again). I was feeling extremely tired and horribly guilty. My husband and I decided to get some help.

We hired someone to come into our home on a regular but part-time basis to help with the children and the house. Ida was such a blessing to our family when I was running my desktop publishing business that I would have taken her with us when we moved if I could have. Having her assistance enabled me to run my business without sacrificing my family. Thanks to Ida, instead of finishing my business work to start on housework, I was able to spend more time with my family, which is the whole point I work at home in the first place.

A friend once asked me if I ever missed cleaning my own house. While I never really get a strong urge to scrub the toilets, I do enjoy taking care of my family and my home. I count it a joy to be able to see to the needs of my children, to make our home a nice place to be, and to be a helpmate to my husband. But I also have to be realistic. When I have a heavy work schedule, I simply need help. Early in my business, there were times when I didn't have any outside help. The kids accompanied me on client deliveries, my then-five-year-old "helped" me clean the house, and Tim mopped floors. Those times made me grateful for the days that I did have domestic help. I think this is one of the biggest mistakes that moms who start businesses make: They don't see the need for domestic help, and they try to add a new business to the full-time job of mothering and home-making. (More on getting help in the next chapter.)

One thing that worked well for me is to share outside help with other people. Regular part-time help can be difficult to find. Several of my friends also needed occasional help with their homes or children, so we all shared Ida's time. She liked it because she was working full-time, and it worked out great for my friends and me, too.

One added advantage was that, since everyone Ida worked for knew each other, we could be flexible about when she worked where.

Set Aside Time to Maintain Your Home

Now that you know what you need to do on a routine basis to keep your household going and what you need help with, decide when you will do it. If you just wait until the mood hits you to do the shopping or scrub the tub, you could be waiting a long time, especially when your business gets busy. Some people like to set aside particular days for particular household maintenance chores (vacuuming on Monday, laundry on Tuesday). Others like to set aside a certain time of each day to do these things ("I'll clean for an hour each morning before I begin working" or "I'll do the shopping in the evenings"). Others—particularly people working at home on a part-time basis—like to set aside one day that is devoted strictly to household duties. That's how Barbara keeps her home managed. "I reserve Monday for 'home day.' We don't plan any activities that day. We go to the grocery store, run all our errands, clean the house, plan the menu for the week, and do the laundry. If something comes up that I really want to do on Monday, I'll take out time the weekend before because my 'home work' really has to be done by Monday night. There is still straightening throughout the week, but if I plan well, most of the work can be done on Monday. I really can't be free of the house if I'm stringing out the work all week."

Things will come up which will occasionally prevent you from sticking to your plan, and many people purposely deviate from their schedule to escape routine. That's fine, but at least creating some kind of plan for accomplishing home maintenance is better than a shot-in-the-dark approach or merely hoping that you'll find the time to fit it all in. Sarah agrees:

"Home is a real priority with me because I really get stressed if it's not organized. You can't do things as they come up like 'Oh, we've run out of clean clothes. We need to wash clothes.' You have to work ahead and be organized. Even though I stress being organized, I'm not a routine person who does certain things on certain days. I do look ahead, though, especially when I'm busy with work, to make time to do things that are needed."

Organize Your Home

If your home lacks organization, now is the best time to get organized. You will need to have your home functioning at its best in order to be able to run a business at the same time. Clean out closets, discover what's under your bed, and be able to locate your personal files quickly. Organize your wardrobe, your kitchen, your cleaning supplies, and your storage system. If you don't have a storage system, try Emilie Barnes' "Total Mess to Total Rest" plan that she details in her books *More Hours in My Day* and *Survival for Busy Women*. Go through your house with a number of large plastic bags and organize your possessions. For each item, either put it away, throw it away, or store it. Store your things in numbered boxes. Make out a three-by-five card listing what you have stored and in which box you put it. Keep these alphabetically listed in a card file. Then you can find whatever you need in seconds. For a more detailed look at organizing your home from stem to stern, read Emilie's books. You will never think the same way about household organization again! After you get everything organized, don't forget to maintain it regularly. This will be your key to an efficiently run home. Besides, who wants to go through the total mess part again? Also, keep the number of your possessions pared down. It's easier to be organized if you have fewer things to organize.

Another way to stay organized and ahead of the game is to do as much as possible before you need it. If you have a morning meeting, lay out your briefcase, papers, or other materials the night before. Also lay out your children's clothes, school things, and lunches the night before.

Take advantage of sales to avoid a last-minute dash to the store for gifts or cards. Keep these treasures set aside on a gift shelf so that you can grab something at a moment's notice for that occasion you forgot or just to save yourself time. Make a list of cards you want to give throughout the year and buy them all at once. Write down these occasions on your calendar. When the birthday rolls around, you won't be making a special trip to the store.

Plan your menus and your grocery list at the same time. Plan for at least a week at a time to avoid impulse purchases and to cut down on trips to the store. I used to go to the store a couple of times a week until I started making out my menus for a month at a time. Now I make my grocery list from that menu and shop at a wholesale club where I buy in bulk. Not only do I save money, but I don't run out of things as quickly. What I can't use right away, I freeze. Then I only have to make a quick trip to the local grocery store once a week for fresh foods. I plan a certain number of meals for the month and pick which meal I feel like having on the day I am going to prepare it. (Relegating particular meals for particular days is a bit too regimented for me.) This frees me not only from running out of things and overspending, but also from standing over my cookbooks wondering what I can fix for dinner.

When possible, try to prepare your meals in advance. One busy home-business owner begins as much of her dinner as possible while she's in the kitchen for breakfast or lunch. If you have a large enough freezer, fix your meals in advance and freeze them. Make double recipes and freeze one meal. Some people like to pick one day a week where they will do several days' worth of cooking. One of the best systems for cooking ahead that I've found is by Jill Bond, and I highly recommend her book *Dinner's in the Freezer*. In it, Jill teaches how to "megacook" for a month at a time (or more!) by making large quantities of certain recipes. Her system can add volumes of time to your life. There have been plenty of evenings when I was grateful, after a hectic day, to have a nice meal ready in minutes thanks to my preparation, my freezer, and my microwave!

Readjust Your Standards

Back to the question of how to get everything done that you did before you had your home business. After you eradicate the nonessential things in your life, garner support and assistance from your family, and hire out some of the tasks you can delegate, you may need to take another step—you may need to readjust your standards in certain areas of your life. "Lower my standards? Never!" you may say. But in the long run you will find that you do indeed need to adjust (if not lower) your standards for the things that don't really matter. Who cares if you have hospital corners on all the beds in your house? Does it really matter that every can in your pantry is stacked alphabetically or all your clothing hangs in your closet according to color? What does count is having your bed made, food in the pantry, and clean clothes in your closet. Decide which standards you will feel comfortable adjusting in order to create more time for your business. Don't lower your standards on the things that are most important to you or your family. But evaluate what really matters and what doesn't. Don't take time away from the things that are important (your relationship with the Lord, your family, your business) to do things that are not such a high priority.

Where Do the Children Fit In?

The room had that "well-lived-in" look. Artboards from a desktop-publishing job were lying on the bed in various stages of completion. A writing project was in front of me as I struggled to edit with one hand and nurse the baby with the other. My five-year-old was singing as she colored on the floor beside me. My two-year-old was blissfully playing in a sinkful of bubbles in the bathroom next to me. From where I was sitting I could see all of this, and I suddenly realized, "So this is how working at home with children can be!" They were looking rather angelic, I was getting something done, and we were all quite happy. I wish I could tell you it's always that much fun or always that easy, but I have to be truthful: Working at home with children, especially young children, is very, well, let's just say...character-building! It can also be fun, rewarding, crazy, loud, silly, trying, and irreplaceable. I wouldn't want to miss a minute of it!

In America today most mothers work. About three fourths of all mothers are in the labor force, according to the U.S. Department of Labor. And moms with very young children are in the work force too—60 percent of them.[1] Statistics also show that the majority of mothers with babies are working, although the good news is that the rate has begun to decline for the first time in decades. A report on children by the Census Bureau showed that the number of children being cared for at home by their married mothers has grown significantly in recent years.[2] That's great news for children and for families.

Of the mothers in the workforce, many would prefer to be with their children. A *Parents* magazine article described the "epidemic" emotional conflict resulting from mothers juggling their jobs and motherhood. One survey of 18,000 women found that only 4 percent of them said they would choose full-time employment if they could "do whatever they wished," and 61 percent of them said they'd choose part-time work if they could. Those attitudes are why so many of the high number of women in the workforce are becoming entrepreneurs.

Along with the fact that so many mothers want to be home with their children, daycare just isn't that great for our kids. The Heritage Foundation put out a widely publicized report that Bill Mattox describes: "It showed that a lot of the most recent data on substitute care arrangements for children disclosed that children who spend a fair amount of time in some type of daycare setting tend to have some negative experiences. This is not an iron rule, but general trends show that kids in those situations often tend to be less attached to their parents, more likely to be engaged in various types of aggression, and often have difficulty in school."[3] That is no news to many of the moms whose children are in daycare. Add to that the difficulty when your children are ill and can't go to the center, when your child cries when you leave, when your child comes home sick from the latest outbreak at the daycare center, and the list goes on.

Sharon is one of the many mothers who does not want her child in daycare: "I want to be able to watch my son grow. In daycare there are so many illnesses, and you don't really know what's going on during the day. By working at home, now I do know, and we're closer than any other situation could allow." Since so many mothers want to be with their children, and so many children want and need to be with their mothers, working at home is becoming a popular solution.

So How Do You Work at Home with Children?

It is possible to work at home with children and continue to be their primary caregiver, but how do you go about it? How do you really run a business with little ones around? I have to divide myself between my children and work, and that's one of the drawbacks. Some people will tell you it cannot be done successfully, at least with any degree of professionalism. Others may tell you it's a breeze. I'll tell you that both are wrong and that, with dedication and the Lord's wisdom, you can do it. You just have to be creative and have a lot of patience, endless energy, and a good supply of crayons! And if you have teenagers, have a good supply of snacks, plenty of gas in the car, and lots of personal availability to listen.

How can you combine the two jobs? One home-worker said, "I cannot put in a full eight-hour day. I have to divide myself between [my son] and work, and that's one of the drawbacks of working at home. I can't give 100 percent to work and 100 percent to my child during the day. But I feel that being with him during the day, having him able to interact with me, is worth dividing myself. I don't have the daycare worries at all, which is worth a lot." Heidi says, "It's a matter of juggling priorities every day. My main priority is to be a good mother for my little girl at home. Sometimes an immediate deadline for a project will take precedence over time that I can spend with her, but I try to juggle things so that I'm not away from her on a full-time basis."

Juggling priorities and sharing time between two jobs is a major part of the solution, but at times your children may have to be in substitute care in order for you to do your job. This type of situation is different from the typical daycare scenario, since avoiding that is one of the reasons you are working at home in the first place. Daycare centers don't even have to be on your option list. Barbara sums it up well: "You have to be flexible. You can't say, 'I'm never going to be away from my child. I'm never going to have any type of daycare.' I think people who say that aren't allowing for any adjustments in their lives. I think you have to go into your business with the attitude, 'What does the Lord want me to do right now?'"

Homeschooling mother and author Luanne Shackelford has said, "We may never get written up in *Redbook* as Wondermom of the Year, but hopefully we will make it through one day, and then another, and then another, and so on until we are old ladies. Then our kids will come back to us and say, 'Mom, I don't know how you ever did it!' and we can look very wise and say, 'Hmm…I did it one day at a time, that's how.'"[4] Although these words were written in reference to homeschooling, they apply to you because you are also attempting to do two things simultaneously: running your business and raising your children. The best way to approach that feat is definitely one day at a time.

One Scripture that has carried me through time and time again is Psalm 68:19: "Blessed be the Lord, who daily bears our burden, the God who is our salvation." Working at home with small children is tough, but God has promised that, as our Lord and Savior, He will carry us through on a day-to-day basis. He has done so for me many, many times.

What Are Your Options?

1. *Share responsibility with your spouse.* Take turns, juggle shifts, and share the load so that you can work while your mate watches the children. This approach works well for women who work part-time, and it helps if your spouse has a somewhat flexible schedule. Talk with your mate and arrange some time off from the kids so you can work in your business.

2. *Pay older siblings to babysit the younger ones.* If you have several children, occasionally hire the oldest to corral the young ones and take them to the park, for walks, to play in the backyard, and supervise them in arts and crafts. The older ones will enjoy earning some money while at the same time learning responsibility. Just be careful of giving older kids too much responsibility. They are still children

themselves. If you need regular care, consider other options, since children need to be raised by adults, not older children.

3. *Barter babysitting time with a friend.* Find someone whom you trust and trade childcare services with her. This is a great option if you can find someone who is available when you need her, who shares your views about what's allowed, and who, in exchange, will let you care for her kids. The best part of this plan is that neither of you is out any money. Some people like this idea because it gives them an opportunity to work undisturbed without the children in the house. If the other family has children who are close in age to yours, they both have playmates.

4. *Hire outside help.* Many people are struggling to make working at home work and can't even consider paying for help. Besides, even if you take working at home out of the picture, it is important to keep expenses down in the start-up phase of most new businesses. However, if you can't get help in other ways, it sometimes becomes imperative to hire part-time help with the children so that you can do your work, call on clients, and deliver goods. For many people, one of the nice things about working at home is that, even if you find that you do have to hire help, you can have your children cared for in your home, where you still get to be near them. Traditional employees do not usually have the option of taking the kids to work. Another plus is that you get to determine if and when and for how long you need childcare help.

Even though parental care is best for children, there may come a time when you just need some help to keep your business going, and that's why I mention various options. Childcare assistance can come in the form of a relative, a neighborhood family daycare setting, a preschool, a mother's-day-out program, and in-home care providers.

a. *A relative.* If you are blessed enough to live in the same area, consider hiring your mother, your grandmother, your sister, or someone else in the family to help you with the children. The children benefit from establishing a closer relationship with that relative than they otherwise might, and you will know your child's caregiver pretty well. Extended families used to be closer, with Grandma often living down the street, but society today tends to spread family members all over the globe. If you are blessed to live close to a relative you feel comfortable having watch your children, and if he or she wants to do it, this may be an ideal option.

b. *A neighborhood family daycare setting.* A family daycare is a place where mothers stay home to care for their children and yours, too. These are not "daycare centers" like the structured programs we talked about before. Instead, childcare is offered in a family/home situation. Some homes take only full-time children, but many will take part-timers and drop-ins. I used this type of childcare when I worked at an "outside" job (and even now occasionally), and the woman I found was a dream. My daughter loved to go to her house and became very close to her children, even sharing birthday celebrations. We shared the same values, and she prayed for my daughter. The local kiddie-corral franchise down the street certainly wouldn't provide this type of care.

c. *A church-sponsored mother's-day-out or preschool.* Many local churches provide drop-in mother's-day-out services where you can take your child for about five hours a day for a very reasonable fee. (The best part of most of these church programs is that your children are taught spiritual values.) You can usually leave your child one or two days a week for mother's-day-out programs and two to three days for preschool programs. Preschools are usually for older children and provide more of a structured learning experience. One woman who uses a mother's-day-out program a few hours a week takes her child to the church 30 minutes earlier than usual before a business meeting. Then she goes back home to finish getting ready, gather her things, and leave with a peaceful heart instead of being totally stressed out. Her child benefits, too, by having a more relaxed mom and more of her attention in the morning.

d. *An in-home care provider.* Hiring someone to come into your home to care for your children is not just a choice for the rich. There are two options: live-out and live-in.

Live-out help might be a teenager, a neighbor, a college student, or an elderly person who needs part-time work. It might be your mother. It could be a childcare-provider/housekeeper who works for you and others on a part-time basis. Or it could be a trained nanny. The options are as varied as the needs that people have. (You may find that your needs change from time to time as well.)

Remember the several ways to find household help mentioned in the last chapter? They can also be a means to find childcare help. Ask your friends if they know of anyone looking for work. Perhaps their helper might want to work for you, too, or they may know of someone else who would. Put an ad on your church bulletin board. Call local churches to see if they know of someone looking for this type of work. Ask your friends or the youth director at your church for reliable sitters.

One home-based worker has found that occasional after-school help is all she needs. "I pay a teenager to come in after school several days a week to play with my child and do odd jobs for me. My child looks forward to when she comes over, and it frees up time for me to work undisturbed."

Going through a nanny service may be the quickest way to find someone (and the service screens the applicants before you interview them), but this is also the costliest option. The one-time fee that the services charge to find you a nanny can run around $1,200 or more for a full-time person. The weekly cost of a nanny is fairly high too, but they are usually quite qualified.

Live-in help can be cheaper than full-time live-out help since you provide room and board. Costs will vary, depending on whether the person speaks English and where you live. For about what it would cost you to have a maid come three half-days, you can usually find a foreign-speaking live-in who would be there full-time. Another live-in source is an *au pair* program: You provide room, board, and a paid vacation for a young woman, usually 18–25 years old, from another country. The weekly salary range varies, but it can be cheaper than full-time childcare in a daycare center, especially if you have several children. Sometimes you pay the airfare here for the *au pair* as well, and she usually stays with the family for a year. *Au pair* programs are often listed in the phone book. A word of caution, though. Some girls from these programs come from countries with extremely liberal cultures, so it might be difficult to find someone who shares your values and beliefs.

One Christian family found a solution through missionary contacts. Working with a missionary family in South America, they paid airfare, room and board, and an allowance for a sweet girl to come to the States and live with them for a year. The girl, cleared by the missionaries, gained invaluable experience, and the family received the help they needed.

For some people in some situations, a live-in might be what they need, particularly if they have a large family or other special needs. Having a full-time person in your home, however, does not mean relegating all authority to the nursemaid and letting someone else raise your kids. It just means that you need help. You do have to be extremely careful when you bring someone into your home, since she will have great influence on your family. You also need to consider whether you have the space and how much privacy your family needs. Some people are very much against this type of help, while others long for it. I am not advocating it, nor do I want to breed discontent in your heart. I just want to present it as an option.

Most home-workers do not need full-time, live-in help, but you may. If so, pray that the person you hire will not only be good for your family, but that your family will be a blessing to her as well. No matter how much help you have (or don't have) with running your home, caring for your children, or running your business, thank the Lord for the blessings He has provided.

Since one of the main reasons many people work at home is to be with their children more, you will often have them around when you're working. If you have preschoolers at home, the picture really gets complicated. Where *do* the children fit in? The following ideas are not meant to take the place of supervised childcare for extended periods of time. After all, young children need constant supervision. These ideas may, however, help keep your children occupied long enough for you to finish that project or make a few business calls.

Tips for Working Around Young Children

1. *Work when they are sleeping.* This is a favorite! You get more done and you *know* they are safe! Try getting up earlier and/or staying up later and working during nap times to get as much done as possible when they are asleep. Stacy combines this with other help as well: "I have my children in mother's-day-out two days a week (a total of ten hours), and I probably get in another hour-and-a-half a day between naps and after bedtime or when they are watching TV, plus another five hours when I have a sitter at the house. I'm probably getting in between 20 and 30 hours a week with my business. There are still plenty of days of McDonald's Happy Meals and afternoons at the park, but on those days I'm usually making phone calls in the morning while they watch 'Sesame Street' and doing paperwork at the desk while they nap."

2. *Provide special toys to play with when you are working.* Set aside a box with toys that they can use only during your work time. Make these "special" toys and frequently change what's in the box. Put surprises in the box from time to time for them to find.

3. *Give them their own "work area" near yours.* Set aside a small area near where you work so they can "work" alongside you. Give them a box or a tray with their own special supplies to be used only during your working hours. Let them have their own envelopes, paper, scissors, crayons, paper clips, tapes, and other office supplies so they can occupy themselves while in your sight. Jacquelyn, my

oldest, loved this when she was little and made hundreds of special creations while we both worked, as have my other children. Years later, my then-four-year-old, Allison, dragged her little desk into my office. As she set herself up with paper and crayons, her desk next to mine, I thought, "Some things never change!"

4. *Fill a sink or plastic tub with sudsy water and lots of Tupperware.* Small children love to wash dishes. If you work close enough to a sink that you can see or hear them, let them wash all the plastic dishes you can find. If not, lay several towels under a plastic tub for dishwashing fun. This can keep some children busy for almost an hour. Sometimes a few puddles are worth 45 minutes to finish a project.

5. *At a table near you, set up special activities for your children.* Let them do puzzles or make paper clip necklaces, paper chains, macaroni art, and so on. Get out the shaving cream and plastic aprons or big T-shirts and let them smear it all over the table. They love this!

6. *Save all your junk mail for them.*

7. *Rotate their toys.* Don't keep all your children's toys out at the same time. Put some of them in boxes or large trash bags and store them. Then once a month or so, bring out the "new" toys and put away some of the ones they have been playing with. This helps keep your children from getting bored with their things.

8. *Keep a cabinet or drawer just for your children.* Fill it with old pots and pans, plastic dishes, or junk odds and ends that you don't mind them playing with. Little ones especially think they are really getting into things, which is often half their fun.

9. *Get special videotapes that they can watch only when you work.* If you have a VCR or DVD player, you can rent or buy videos or DVDs and bring them out only occasionally to keep them "special." Many productions are educational and entertaining, and many excellent Christian videos and DVDs are available as well. To save money, record PBS specials, Christmas specials, and other good family

viewing. If you have opted to get rid of your television, you can buy special monitors that do not receive TV signals. This way you can control what your family watches.

10. *Use monitored TV.* I'm not talking about plunking your kids in front of the tube for an afternoon of "Teenage Mutant Ninja Turtles" and "Ghostbusters." TV can be harmful to children, which is why it is so important to monitor what they watch and to limit the time they are allowed to watch it. What good does it do to work at home if the little ones are glued to the boob tube for hours on end? However, many people have found that occasional viewing isn't so terrible. But be warned: "Good" TV is often linked with bad commercials! If you can't be in the room when your children are watching TV, stick to PBS or DVDs. Just don't get dependent on the TV to babysit the kids. It's easy to do when you work at home, but costly for your children.

11. *Buy a two-gallon cooler with a push-button spout and paper cups.* Keep this in the kitchen within reach so the kids can help themselves. This can save you hundreds of trips to the kitchen!

Other Tips for Working at Home with Children

1. *Set ground rules.* It is important to establish a set of rules that will work for you and your family. Make it clear to your children what you expect, what is allowed, and what is not allowed while you are working. If you have business hours, make sure your children know this. Let them know what things they may touch and which areas are hands-off. Are they allowed to answer the phone? (This is not a good idea if your business line is also your home number, and clients will be calling.) Can they answer only during certain times? Tell your children what you expect of them when you are on a business call. If you don't tell them, most children will still ask you for a drink and cry for justice when sister takes their favorite toy no matter if you are on the phone to the president! (Incidentally, phone

silencers are made that cut out background noise when the other party is talking.) Are they allowed to interrupt your work whenever they want to, or do you have "Do Not Disturb" times?

I have tried to establish an open door/shut door policy from the time my oldest was very young through today, with minor modifications. It used to go something like this: "When Mommy's office door is shut that means I'm working. If my door is open that means you may come in and I will be happy to talk with you. Unless someone is bleeding or the house is on fire, please ask Daddy instead of knocking on my door." When my oldest was five and my second child was two, that policy was a little tough to implement, especially since I could usually only shut my door if my husband was home. Today it's much easier. I use hand signals when I'm on the phone. A palm out sign means, "You may not disturb me." A beckoning sign when I'm on the phone means, "This phone call's not urgent. Quietly come in." Hand signals in tandem with the door rules work well. It lets my children know when they absolutely may not disturb me without me being rude or ignoring them. I want my children to feel welcome but also to completely respect when I'm working.

A writer friend of mine has another good rule that I like to use, too. The children are never allowed to walk into the office talking. I could be doing a radio interview or I might be deep into writing.

The only exception to all the rules is if someone is hurt. I add, "And I better see gushing blood, too!" (I think they see through that, though.)

Finally, if you expect your children to obey your rules while you are working, make certain that they know what the rules are in advance and be consistent as you implement them.

2. *Include your children in your work when you can.* Including your children in your work whenever possible makes your children feel more a part of your life. When Daddy goes off to the office day after day, how many children really understand what Daddy does? When Daddy works at home, children can better understand how Daddy spends his time, especially if he makes an effort to include his

children whenever possible. Depending on the nature of your business and the ages of your children, there are many ways to involve your kids in your work. Let them stuff envelopes, help box products, or accompany you on business errands or deliveries. One mother who has a baking business said, "My children now know what it takes to get food on the table. They see that baked goods don't just come from the grocery store. They've helped me make the things I sell and have seen the process needed to get them there." Your children can learn skills and the value of hard work. They can learn responsibility while nurturing family bonds. You will have the opportunity to teach and influence them not only by what you are doing but also by the way you work and the attitude you have about your work. If your children see you "working as unto the Lord," they will have someone to emulate. Involving our children can produce spiritual growth in their lives as well as our own.

3. *Schedule breaks with your children.* Stop working periodically to spend some time with your children. If they are at home while you're working, stop for a few minutes. Read a story. Build a Lego building. Color a picture. Play with paper dolls. It may take only 15 minutes, but the break will do both you and your child good. Besides, how many nine-to-fivers do you know who can fingerpaint in the middle of the day? If your children are being cared for away from your home, plan on a break when you can be together and they can have your undivided attention. And don't refuse to allow unplanned breaks. Sometimes your children really need you now, not in 30 minutes. If your child keeps interrupting you, stop. Maybe all he really wants is a hug and 60 seconds in your lap before he's off to play again.

4. *Implement a "kids' time."* Set aside a special time of the day for your children that is just for them. Maybe midmorning is craft time. Perhaps just before naptime is story hour. Maybe you have a special snack and a listening ear when your kids come home from school. When your children know that you make time for them just as you do

for your business, they will be less likely to resent the time you spend working. Even if you work full-time at home, you can make "kids' time" a habit that you and your children love. Sometimes when my girls and I are engrossed in something together during our special time and the phone rings, my daughter will say, "Mommy, please let the machine get it!"—and I do. On occasion a deadline may prevent you from having this extended one-on-one time with your children, but that can be the exception instead of the norm. If you work only part-time, then spending time with the children may not be as great a problem. But full-time work at home and a growing business can—if we aren't careful—make it difficult to spend with our children the kind and amount of time we want to, especially since we cannot leave our work to "go home."

5. *Plan a special activity or outing.* Plan something special to do with your children (or as a family) each week or month or whenever suits your family. Mark it on the calendar so your children can see when this will happen. Go skating. Take a walk. Have a picnic. Go to a museum. Do something fun with your kids and involve them in deciding what you will do. You might even let this be a special reward for following your "work-at-home rules."

6. *Let your children know when you will be finished working.* Time is a difficult thing for young children to grasp, and not knowing when you will be done is frustrating for kids who always seem to want you now. So when they ask when you'll be finished, don't say "soon" or "later." Give them a time and honor your word. If your children are too young to tell time, set a timer and tell them you'll be done when the bell rings. Or say, "When this big hand is on the 12" or "When Mr. Rogers is over" or "When the numbers on the clock say three zero zero." Perhaps if they know when you will be finished, they won't keep coming in every five minutes to ask if you're done yet.

7. *Pray for your children often.* Pray for their safety and protection while you work. Pray that they will learn and grow from your business experience and that it will be a positive influence in their lives. Pray

that the children will see God working in your life and in your business and that they will grow spiritually.

Fitting children into a work-at-home routine is certainly not the easy path; it is definitely a challenge. It takes creativity, forethought, and effort to be able to work at home when you have children. It also takes a sense of humor. When my second child was two years old, she was quite attached to her "blankie," but if it didn't happen to be available, anything silky would suffice. (Consequently, I considered getting a padlock for my lingerie drawer!) My husband and I were desperately trying to get her to break this habit. But one day I was in the back of the house when the doorbell rang. I opened the door and a client of mine stepped into the entryway. Out of the corner of my eye and directly behind him, I saw the contents of that lingerie drawer strewn all over the floor of my recently neat den. I quickly escorted my unsuspecting guest into the kitchen, asked him to please have a seat, and fast and furiously gathered my belongings. After he left I tried to explain to my little one that what she had done was a no-no. A short while later I had to drop some work off at another client's office. I conducted my business and left the office, but as I was walking across the parking lot toward my car, I looked down and saw a remnant from that lingerie escapade sticking telltale out of my boot. (Guess who had been playing at my feet!) My red face and I drove away...quickly.

Even though you sometimes have to struggle to maintain a level of professionalism and use all the ingenuity you have to work at home with kids around, it is still fun. And it is worth it. At times when my children have had to be in the care of someone other than myself for any length of time, I realized how much I would miss them if that were the norm. My heart bleeds for the vast number of women who want to be home with their children but can't because they have outside jobs.

When my children were babies, I loved being able to have them with me. I loved taking a break from my work and helping them with their smiles and coos. Thinking of friends who told me that they had to go back to work when their babies were six weeks old, I would look at my little ones and be so thankful that I did not have to do the same. Being available to my older children, teenagers, and daughter when she is home from college is every bit as important as being home when they were small. I am so grateful that my heavenly Father has made it possible for me to work at home. If you are struggling with the decision to take this same step, I pray that God will guide you along the right path for your family.

If you have very young children or a big family, remember that your load is heavier than most, but you don't have to go it alone. If you feel that the Lord is leading you toward working at home, remember that He promises to bear your burdens daily. Psalm 113:9 says, "He makes the barren woman abide in the house as a joyful mother of children. Praise the Lord!" Not only does this verse talk about answered prayer for the childless, but it describes a woman who abided at home with her children around—and she was *happy* about it!

So try not to think about how long it will be before your baby is in school so you can really get some work done or how much easier it is for so-and-so, whose older children don't require constant supervision. The time we have with our children goes by all too quickly. We are accountable for what we do with that time to make a difference for eternity in our children. Jean Fleming said in her book *A Mother's Heart,* "I have no regrets about the years I have spent as a full-time wife and mother. The aspect of mothering that excites me most is the knowledge that I am making a permanent difference in my children's lives."

Working from home has allowed me to accomplish just that—to make "a permanent difference in my children's lives." However, let's look at Mrs. Fleming's comment again: "I have no regrets about the years I have spent as a *full-time* wife and mother" (emphasis mine). I want to clarify that I am not advocating that all, or even most, mothers begin home businesses. If you have the opportunity to be a full-time homemaker while your children are young, that is an invaluable and very fulfilling role. It is less stressful and probably easier on you and your children to be a full-time mom rather than trying to combine parenting with home-based work. I have always been quick to say that working at home with young children is one of the toughest roads to travel. Emotionally, of course, it's much easier than outside work. But in a straight comparison, focusing on only the children is much simpler than focusing on the children and a business. That is why for several years in between my desktop publishing and my writing and speaking business, I chose to focus solely on my family. That is why now my work is part-time. I could very easily increase my work hours, income, and achievements, but I choose not to…for now.

I remember reading an article years ago that featured a mother of four wondering what kind of business she could start at home. The writer responded, "With four kids, you don't need a home business." At the time, I thought, "How can that writer discourage her like that?" But experience and having more children have shown me that those words held much truth. I have found that working from home with five children isn't the same thing as working from home with two. However, as children get older, working from home gets easier. Having my teenagers around has been much easier than working with preschoolers was, for they've been an invaluable source of help. Even so, I enjoyed the years when I focused only on raising my children. I'm enjoying my part-time work now, and I look forward to an increased career in my empty-nest season, but like Mrs. Fleming, I want to be able to say that I have no regrets.

My advice to you then? Follow your heart and God's leading. If full-time motherhood is really more appealing to you than being a businesswoman and if you can afford it financially, choose motherhood because children grow up so fast. Then, instead of starting a business, maybe you can find a way to cut expenses. Doing so might serve your family better than generating more income. The late Larry Burkett's ministry, Crown Financial Ministries, is a great resource for tips. If you're considering starting a business, but this little "motherhood disclaimer" sends a warning signal, listen. If my words here dissuade someone who's not suited for working from home, then this book has accomplished its other purpose.

But for the countless women who seriously desire home-based work, then I encourage you. Some women need the stimulation, creative outlet, and career opportunities that working from home allows. Others need the income. And millions are opting for the advantages of increased parent time/decreased caregiver time for the children. Working from home is a way to bring in an income and still make that eternal difference Mrs. Fleming was talking about, without depending on "quality time" before and after an outside job.

If you're wondering whether you will be able to work with your kids around, just take a big breath, pray for patience and inspiration, and accept the challenge with joy. It's worth it!

14

Keeping
First Things First

Certain things in life demand our greatest attention and wholehearted devotion: our relationship with the Lord, our relationship with our spouse and our children, and, after these relationships, our work. Working at home provides an excellent opportunity to make a living while living out these priorities. Although working at home certainly isn't the easiest route to take, it can mean immeasurable blessings. In fact, God can use your home business in ways that you never dreamed possible to teach you spiritual truths and life-changing lessons.

Now there will be days when you get started at the crack of dawn and find yourself working long after you had planned to stop. And there will be days when nothing seems to go right: the children are demanding, your spouse is demanding—and your clients need you, too. You may feel guilty about lack of time and energy for your family, your household responsibilities, and/or your work. You may even ask yourself why you started the business in the first place.

Even on those occasional days, you can be victorious as the Lord sustains you. Home-worker Barbara knows of God's faithfulness especially during those rough times: "Whenever I wonder if this is all worth it, the Lord reconfirms it in small ways."

Working at home is not for everyone. First of all, not everyone has the temperament or even the desire to start a business of their own.

Many do not have the necessary support from their family. Others do not have the energy level or drive to make it happen. And some simply are not called to do it.

If you don't feel that the Lord has called you to work at home, don't even try it. Without His guidance in your endeavor or your commitment to follow His leading in your life, you could end up a broken-business statistic. Doug Sherman and William Hendricks say in *Your Work Matters to God*, "Unless you can make a connection between what you do all day and what you think God wants you to be doing, you will never find ultimate meaning in your work or in your relationship with God." Don't just start a business for the sake of having a business. Know beforehand that what you are doing is part of the Lord's plan for your life.

Lessons in Trust

For Christians, being an entrepreneur is an ongoing lesson in trusting God. He has used Heidi's business to help her and her husband learn to trust Him more. She explains, "My business hasn't taken off extremely well in terms of superabundance coming in, but it's taught us a lot about relying on the Lord. Sometimes just in the nick of time some business will come in. I'm not the super-sales-person, and I tend to want to stay home more than go out and solicit business, so God's hand has really been evident in bringing business in. God has taught us trust."

The blessing of developing a greater trust in our heavenly Father—and other blessings along the way—can overshadow the problems that come with home businesses. These blessings can lift us up, lighten our load, strengthen our faith, and teach us more about the nature of our Creator as He gives to us from His storehouse. Working from my home has been exciting because I have seen the Lord work in my life in very concrete ways. I have found, for instance, that the Lord has a way of hearing our innermost desires even when we don't fall on our knees and fervently petition Him. Let me explain.

First, some home-workers run into trouble because they don't work in their businesses as much as they need to, while others work too much. At times I have fallen into both categories. The Lord used one of those "too much" times once to teach me a few things—some things I'm glad I learned early on in my home-business days.

My desktop publishing had taken off like gangbusters, and I was extremely busy. As the business grew, I had less time available to be the kind of wife and mother I desired. Without realizing how it happened or knowing how I could get off the whirlwind track, I had become immersed in my business. Oh, I still had opportunities to make cookies, read books, and play with the kids (two days a week I was both full-time Mom and home-business owner), but their place on my priority list had slipped. I was leaving those fun times with the kids for my "free" time, after I'd met all my business obligations. Sometimes, in the middle of chocolate-chip cookie batter and preschool chatter, I would find myself dwelling on my latest project instead of enjoying the moment with my kids.

Furthermore, since I am a pretty motivated, ambitious person by nature (as are many entrepreneurs), my work was never done. I always came up with something else to do regarding the business, and this preoccupation was changing the nature of my time with the children. Gradually I began to notice that on the three weekdays that our housekeeper/babysitter came, I went into my office and said, "Mommy has to work now; go ask Miss Ida"—even if there wasn't a deadline looming. As I saw this happening, I hated it, but I wasn't sure how to change it. I reasoned, "If Ida is going to be here, I need to get as much done as possible. If I work while she's here, I can increase my business, which we need, and I can still have free time with the kids when I'm done. Besides, I'm home with them. It's not like I'm off at an office or anything."

Realigning Those Priorities

As I began to see how needing to work in the business was affecting both the quality and quantity of time with my children, I felt stuck. How could I slow down when we needed the money? How would my husband feel? And how did he feel about things now? Tim didn't really see anything wrong. Because my helper was here so much, the house was always clean, the meals were served on time, and he always had clean underwear (which wasn't always the case when I was trying to do everything myself). What Tim couldn't see was the time I spent in the same house with the children but was totally removed from what they were doing or feeling—all for the sake of the business. I began to pray for a way to be a better mother and to live according to the values I treasure. The Lord knew the desire of my heart and went ahead of me.

Slowly, my clients began to drop off one by one. As far as I could tell, I wasn't doing anything differently to warrant this decrease, but I had fewer and fewer jobs. The housekeeper was no longer affordable because, with less business, there was less money. On the other hand, the less business I had, the more time I had. Business consultants would probably have told me to invest that time in my business and promote my company back into success, but I didn't. I had been wanting to spend more time with my children anyway, so I was thrilled to have an excuse to be with them more. I began to get reacquainted with Slap Jack and Candyland!

My five-year-old and I started doing housework together, something we had previously done as quickly as possible. She collected and sorted laundry, cleaned the tub, washed the mirrors (and her babies' faces) with Windex, ran the vacuum cleaner for the first time, learned how to use a dustpan, saw how much soap is used for a load of laundry, and helped with an assortment of other tasks. For her this was a fun new game. I was ashamed that I had taken so little time before to teach her these things and to do them with her at a relaxed pace.

The kids also began to accompany me—often. They occasionally went with me to client meetings and learned quickly what was acceptable behavior and what wasn't. On one trip that involved an extremely long wait, we used the time to talk and read books. Right when I thought they were going to lose their patience with the wait, Jacquelyn looked up at me and said, "Mom, you're fun!" My heart melted. All that my children really wanted was my time, and I had been far too stringent with the amount I gave them. I praised God that He had brought me back to what was important by slowing down my business.

For my husband and me, this was a lesson in trust and a call to live our priorities, because even though I now had more "Mommy-time," we still needed the income. Facing a possible business loss is a scary thing, and the thought of getting an outside job with daycare for the kids was even scarier. But instead of getting ulcers about losing the business, we decided to take Paul's advice: "Be anxious for nothing, but in everything by prayer and supplication with thanksgiving let your requests be made known to God" (Philippians 4:6).

Keeping First Things First

We began to pray that the Lord would meet our financial needs and direct us regarding the business. I'd like to tell you that we prayed and I got ten new regular clients the next day or we won the Publisher's Clearinghouse sweepstakes, but neither happened. Instead we waited several months before really seeing God's answer to our prayers, but the Lord used that time to show us that He would meet our needs on a daily basis. I had no doubt that the Lord had cleared my slate, and I realized later that He had done so for some things that were coming in my life. I would never have been able to orchestrate the timing of the events or organize the details as God did. He also knew that I needed the time to make my children a top priority again and to be available for future tasks. God taught me that I had been depending on my business to make ends meet instead of on Him. I also learned that what really mattered was my obedience and availability to the Lord and my time with my family.

Now here's where the miracle part comes in. All of a sudden—and with no effort on my part—I began to get new business. I had actually gotten down to zero clients (now that's rock bottom!) when the phone began to ring again. Strangely, every single job I received was through word-of-mouth advertising and not a result of anything I had done. My business income was double that of previous months, and I knew the increase was truly from the Lord.

It's difficult for me to admit that I had trouble making time for my children the way I should have and that my business has been less than the "home-business model," but I think I struggle with some of the same things you do. It's very easy to have your priorities in place; it's another thing to live them. Even if you don't have children, be careful to keep your priorities in place and, more importantly, to live them out. Make time for the things in life that really matter. Having a home business is not always easy, and sometimes it's downright tough. But when we seek the Lord and His direction, He will see us through and, in both adversity and victory, teach us.

Success Is from God

One home-worker shares this lesson, which she has realized in her business again and again: "No matter how hard I push, I can't make things happen unless it's the Lord's will. I'm finally approaching the business the way we should approach everything in life. I'm going to be obedient to the Lord, but what happens beyond that is His business. He can do it, but I can't."

In a letter to "Focus on the Family" radio talkshow listeners, Dr. James Dobson also acknowledges the Lord's role in the accomplishments of His people: "Egos being what they are, the natural inclination is to take personal credit for any successes coming our way. But we know the dangers of that error. Every positive thing that has happened in our history has been a direct consequence of God's blessing. If He ever removes His hand of mercy from us, we would flounder helplessly in a sea of futility."[1]

Those of us who start home businesses also need God's "hand of mercy." After all, we value our roles as wife, mother, and homemaker. Each of these roles is as important as ever even if you decide to work out of your home. You will need to make some adjustments in how you live them out, but becoming a businessperson in your own home doesn't preclude those other important jobs.

Titus 2:5 tells us that we must be "sensible, pure, workers at home, kind, being subject to [our] own husbands, that the word of God may not be dishonored." Study the godly woman in Proverbs 31. She would have fit in nicely in this decade, for she was on the move and got things done. She cooked, served, bought real estate, invested, and helped the needy. She was a seamstress, a beltmaker, and a mother much loved by her children. Yet she remained a virtuous woman, an excellent wife. Let her be your role model.

Another thing. If you feel the Lord is leading you to begin working at home, but are fearful because of a previous business failure or past mistakes, don't let that alone hinder you from beginning. Successful people also have failures—lots of them. The legendary Babe Ruth struck out 1,330 times, yet ended up being one of the greatest home-run hitters in the history of baseball! If you've struck out, don't dwell on past errors. "Brethren, I do not regard myself as having laid hold of it yet; but one thing I do; forgetting what lies behind and reaching forward to what lies ahead..." (Philippians 3:13).

True Commitment

The cornerstone of home-business success is based on one word: commitment. Commitment to the business and, more importantly, to the Lord.

If we are not committed to the work we do, we flounder. Without being dedicated to the work, we are simply marking time instead of learning, growing, and prospering. Commitment means work. Commitment demands our energy, our time, our concentration, and our determination to succeed. If commitment came easily, we wouldn't see the tremendous number of divorces that we do. So be committed to your work, not just to reaping the benefits, but because your work really does matter to God.

First and foremost, however, we must commit our work, our goals, and our lives to the Lord. The Bible has a lot to say about commitment. When I was starting my business, one of the most meaningful verses was Proverbs 16:3: "Commit your works to the Lord, and your plans will be established." My business is God's, to be used for His glory. Psalm 37:3-5 tells us, "Trust in the Lord, and do good; dwell in the land and cultivate faithfulness. Delight yourself in the Lord, and He will give you the desires of your heart. Commit your way to the Lord, trust also in Him, and He will do it." The psalmist calls us to trust and delight in the Lord and to commit our goals to Him. If we do, God will plant in our heart His desires for us, and when we desire what He desires for us, He does indeed bless us. Most important, we are to commit our lives to Him, and that means naming Him our Savior and Lord. If you have never done that, I pray that before you consider anything else, you consider Jesus. He wants a personal relationship with you, and He will actively intervene in your life if you invite Him in. I encourage you to make a difference not only in your business but also in your eternal future by committing yourself to Him—by acknowledging your sinfulness, asking God to forgive you, and then naming Jesus as your Lord as well as your Savior.

As you begin your journey into the realm of home-business, you will learn and you will grow, but most of all you will realize the power of the Lord at work in your life like never before. Be attuned to all the miracles that God will do for you that you might otherwise miss. If you really feel the Lord leading you to begin a business, He will amaze you with the direct interaction He lovingly gives when you ask Him. God cares about the very smallest detail in our lives.

Remember that working at home is an adventure to be all that you can for the Lord. Commit your work to Him, and He will establish your plans. Let that be the motto of your enterprise. If you have doubts along the way (and you will), rest in the Lord. If you have fears about what you are doing (and you may), trust in your heavenly Father. When you see victories, give God the praise. Let working at home be a way to honor and serve the Lord. Allow God to use your work at home to make your family life, your personal life, your work life, and your spiritual life all that He wants it to be. Most of all, remember that God sees possibilities above all that we ask or think (Ephesians 3:20).

I pray that the Lord will bless you in your new endeavor!

"May He grant you your heart's desire and fulfill all your counsel" (Psalm 20:4).

Resources

Where to Go for Help

A wealth of information is available to help you start or grow a home-based business. Your top three tools to help you gain the ongoing information you need are the Internet, the public library, and bookstores. On the Internet, you can access most of the resources in this section quickly via their websites. I've predominantly listed only websites for the following resources since addresses and phone numbers can change and you can always do a websearch for the resource if the URL changes. The Internet is also the tool to locate information specific to your business needs with a google.com search or other search engine, and amazon.com to quickly find new and older books. Use your second resource tool, the library, to become acquainted with the reference librarians (they are a gold mine of information) or to go online if you don't have a home computer. You can also do searches at the library (online or CD-ROM) for indexed information from business periodicals, consumer publications, and databases of major newspaper articles. Your third information tool is your local bookstore, where you can find the newest releases of business books—and maybe even a great latté.

Community Sources of Information

Local libraries, colleges, universities, chambers of commerce, local business organizations, and local chapters of national organizations can provide plenty of information for digging.

State Assistance

Most states have agencies that promote economic growth by assisting small businesses. Some states specifically address home business issues. Many states also publish guides to starting a business in their states. Your state's Department of Agriculture and your state's Department of Health are the agencies to contact for information regarding food-related businesses. Look in the phone directory under "State Government."

Federal Information

Copyright Office—The Library of Congress, www.loc.gov

Internal Revenue Service—www.irs.gov

Enter the IRS site's search line with the following phrases for helpful information and links to related forms:

✓ Business Use of Your Home
✓ Employee or Independent Contractor
✓ Recordkeeping

Small Business Administration—www.sba.gov

The U.S. Small Business Administration (SBA) offers assistance to those in small business by providing information about starting, financing, and managing your business; obtaining government contracts; and disaster recovery. Most local offices provide free business start-up kits. Some offices offer informative seminars. Look in the "Government" section of your phone book for your local SBA office or locate it at their website. You can also obtain the SBA publication

The Business Plan for Home-Based Business by typing MP-15 in the SBA site's search line.

SBA's Small Business Development Centers—www.sba.gov/sbdc/

These centers, usually associated with colleges and universities, provide prospective and existing small-business owners with various assistance. SBDC says its program "is designed to deliver up-to-date counseling, training and technical assistance in all aspects of small business management. SBDC services include, but are not limited to, assisting small businesses with financial, marketing, production, organization, engineering and technical problems, and feasibility studies."

SCORE (Service Corps of Retired Executives)—www.score.org

SCORE, also known as "Counselors to America's Small Business," is a nonprofit association dedicated to providing entrepreneurs with free, confidential face-to-face and e-mail business counseling. Hundreds of chapter offices across the country offer business counseling and workshops.

Patent and trademark information—www.uspto.gov

The Patent and Trademark office is part of the U.S. Department of Commerce.

Better Business Bureau—www.bbb.org

At this site you can check out a company or charity, file a complaint, or get interesting consumer information.

Trade Associations

A trade association is a group largely comprised of business people within a particular industry or service area. Such associations offer networking, information about industry developments or trends, specialized publications or information in their fields, and sometimes federal or state information regarding their specializations. Check the *Encyclopedia of Associations* at your library for groups in your industry or service. You might also try an online search for associations within a category or group. The American Society of Association Executives (ASAE) has a searchable directory of associations at http://info.asaenet.org/find/ that you may find useful.

Business Associations

American Home Business Association—www.homebusiness.com

American Woman's Economic Development Corporation—www.awed.org

National Association for the Self-Employed—www.nase.org

National Association of Women Business Owners—www.nawbo.org

National Chamber of Commerce for Women—www.uswomenschamber.com

National Federation of Business and Professional Women's Clubs, Inc.—www.bpwusa.org

Women Entrepreneurs—www.we-inc.org

Magazines, Newsletters, and Home Business Organizations

Entrepreneur Magazine—www.entrepreneur.com

EWorking Women—www.eworkingwomen.com

Family and Home Network—www.familyandhome.org

Fortune Small Business Magazine—www.fsb.com

Home-Based Working Moms—www.hbwm.com

Home Business Magazine—www.homebusinessmag.com

Home Business Report—www.homebusinessreport.com

Home Work Magazine—www.momshomework.com

Mothers' Home Business Network—www.homeworkingmom.com

Wall Street Journal Center for Entrepreneurs—www.startupjournal.com

Books, Websites, and Recordings

Blasingame, Jim. *Small Business Is Like a Bunch of Bananas.* Florence, AL: SBN Books, 2001. www.jbsba.com

Bond, Jill. *Mega Cooking.* Nashville: Cumberland House, 2000. And *Dinner's in the Freezer.* Great Christian Books, 1994. www.bondingplace.com

Brabec, Barbara. *Homemade Money: Starting Smart.* New York: M. Evans & Co., 2003. www.barbarabrabec.com

Burkett, Larry. *Business by the Book: Complete Guide of Biblical Principles for the Workplace.* Nashville: Thomas Nelson, 1998. See also Crown Financial Ministries. www.crown.org

Demas, Cheryl. *It's a Jungle Out There and a Zoo in Here.* New York: Warner, 2003. www.wahm.com

Edwards, Paul and Sarah, and Peter Economy. *Why Aren't You Your Own Boss?* New York: Prima Publishing, 2003. www.homeworks.com

Focus on the Family (www.family.org), audio recording: *Home Employment: Exploring the Options.* This is a recording of a two-day broadcast with Dr. James Dobson, featuring a panel of Posy Lough (www.posycollection.com), Brenda Koinis (www.theh2oproject.com), and me (Lindsey O'Connor) (www.lindseyo.com).

Folger, Liz. *The Stay-at-Home Mom's Guide to Making Money from Home.* New York: Prima Publishing, 2000. www.bizymoms.com

Fuller, Cheri. *Home Business Happiness.* Colorado Springs: Starburst, 1996. www.cherifuller.com

Horowitz, Shel. *Marketing Without Megabucks.* Northampton, MA: AMW Books, 2003. www.frugalmarketing.com

Hunt, Mary. *The Financially Confident Woman.* Nashville: Broadman and Holman, 1996. www.cheapskatemonthly.com

Kamoroff, Bernard. *Small-Time Operator: How to Start Your Own Small Business, Keep Your Books, Pay Your Taxes, and Stay Out of Trouble!* Laytonville, CA: Bell Springs Publishing, 2000. www.bellsprings.com

Levine, Michael and George Gendron. *Guerilla P.R. Wired.* New York: McGraw-Hill, 2001. www.levinepr.com

Levison, Jay and Seth Godin. *Guerilla Marketing Handbook.* Boston: Mariner, 1994. www.gmarketing.com

Notes

Chapter I—Working at Home: Beyond a Trend

1. Bill Mattox, The Heritage Foundation, personal interview.
2. Ellen H. Parlapiano and Patricia Cobe, *Mompreneurs: A Mother's Practical Step-by-Step Guide to Work-at-Home Success* (New York, NY: Berkley Publishing Group, 1997), p. 2.
3. "The Mommy Track: Juggling Kids and Corporate America Takes a Controversial Turn," in *Business Week*, Mar. 20, 1989, p. 127.
4. Parlapiano and Cobe, *Mompreneurs*, p. 5.
5. Mattox, personal interview.
6. Paul and Sarah Edwards, *Working from Home: Everything You Need to Know About Living and Working Under the Same Roof* (Los Angeles: J.P. Tarcher, Inc., 1985), p. 13.

Chapter 3—Making the Decision

1. Mary Pride, *All the Way Home* (Westchester, IL: Crossway Books/Good News, 1989), p.188.
2. Ibid., p. 187.
3. Ingrid Kindred, "Trend of the '80s: Never Leaving Home to Go to Work," in *Birmingham News*, Oct. 6, 1986.
4. Jerome Goldstein, *In Business for Yourself* (New York: Charles Scribner's Sons, 1982), p. 26.

5. Edith Flowers Kilgo, *Money in the Cookie Jar* (Grand Rapids: Baker Book House, 1980), p. 31.

Chapter 5—Setting Up Your Business

1. "Zero in on Reality," in *Nation's Business*, Oct. 1988, p. 37.

2. Barbara Brabec, *Homemade Money: Your Homebased Business Success Guide for the '90s*, rev. ed. (Crozet, VA: Betterway Publications, 1992).

3. *Legal Aspects of Small Business* (American Entrepreneurs Association, 1984), pp. 3305-12.

4. Ibid., pp. 3305-15.

5. Ibid., pp. 3303-05.

6. Ibid., pp. 3305-07,

7. Ingrid Kindred, "Trend of the '80s: Never Leaving Home to Go to Work," in *Birmingham News*, Oct. 6, 1986.

8. *Home Offices and Workspaces* (Menlo Park, CA: Sunset Books, Lane Publishing Co., 1986), p. 39.

9. Roger Ricklefs and Udayan Gupta, "Traumas of a New Entrepreneur," in *The Wall Street Journal*, May 10, 1989.

Chapter 6—Marketing: The One Thing You Can't Do Without

1. David F. Ramacitti, *Do-It-Yourself Marketing* (New York: AMACOM, 1994), pp. 1, 2, 7.

2. Ellen H. Parlapiano and Patricia Cobe, *Mompreneurs: A Mother's Practical Step-by-Step Guide to Work-at-Home Success* (New York: Berkley Publishing Group, 1997), p.199.

3. Jay Conrad Levinson, *Guerrilla Marketing Attack* (Boston, MA: Houghton Mifflin, 1989), p.121.

4. Ramacitti, *Do-It-Yourself*, p. 108.

Chapter 7—Home Business Online

1. Different forums will have different acronyms for quick communication. You'll find some in the Christian sub-net to be "dh" for *dear husband;* "lol" for *laughing out loud,* "pmfji" *for pardon me for jumping in.* Shorthand like this saves typing and speeds up responses.

2. Netiquette refers to the agreed-upon rules for online behavior (e.g., writing in all capital letters is the same as shouting and considered very RUDE—and doing so can get you booted out of some forums).

3. Emoticons are symbols that communicate emotions. Since you are typing, others can't hear the joy or laughter in your voice, so Web-sters have developed

shorthand ways of displaying emotions quickly—e.g., :) symbolizes a smiling face (look at it sideways) while :(is a frown and \o/ is "Praise the Lord!"

4. Web-sters is one of the many terms for those who are online. Some others are websites, surfers, chatters, and netheads.

Chapter 8—Telecommuting

1. "How Corporate America Takes Its Work Home," in *Modem Office Technology,* July 1989.

2. International Telework Assoc. and Connect, as quoted at Home-Based Working Moms, hbwm.com, Aug. 2003.

3. Electronic Commerce and Telework Trends, as quoted at Home-Based Working Moms, hbwm.com, Aug. 2003.

4. "How Corporate America Takes Its Work Home," p. 54.

5. *Tips on Work-at-Home Schemes,* Consumer Information Series (Council of the Better Business Bureau).

Chapter 10—Managing Your Business

1. "Idea from" Paul and Sarah Edwards, *Working from Home* (Los Angeles: J.P. Tarcher, Inc., 1987), p. 226.

2. Davis Bushnell, "Home Offices Not Always Heaven," in *Boston Globe,* Sep. 12, 1988.

Chapter 11—Managing Your Time

1. Idea learned from Donna Clark Goodrich, *How to Set up and Run a Typing Service* (New York: John Wiley and Sons, 1983), p. 18.

2. Emilie Barnes, *The Creative Home Organizer* (Eugene, OR: Harvest House Publishers, 1988), p.15.

3. Nicole Wise, "Successful Strategies for Part-Time Work," in *Parents,* Dec. 1988, p. 71.

4. Jim Trelease, *The Read Aloud Handbook* (New York: Penguin Books, 1982), p. 99.

Chapter 12—Managing Your Home

1. James Dobson, *Fatigue and the Homemaker* (Arcadia, CA: "Focus on the Family" booklet, 1986).

2. Luanne Shackelford and Susan White, *A Survivor's Guide to Homeschooling* (Westchester, IL: Crossway Books, 1988), p. 36.

Chapter 13—Where Do the Children Fit In?

1. U.S. Dept. of Labor, Bureau of Labor Statistics, online statistics, bls.gov, Aug. 2003.

2. Cheryl Wetzstein, "More kids cared for by moms at home," *Washington Times,* June 16, 2003, washtimes.com.

3. Interview with Bill Mattox formerly of the Family Research Council.

4. Shackelford and White, *A Survivor's Guide to Homeschooling,* pp. 106-07.

Chapter 14—Keeping First Things First

1. Dr. James Dobson, "Focus on the Family" letter, Oct. 1989, p. 2.

Index

Other Books by Lindsey O'Connor

If Mama Goes South, We're All Going with Her

If Mama Ain't Happy, Ain't Nobody Happy

Moms Who Changed the World

જી

For more information on these books and Lindsey
O'Connor's speaking topics and availability, go to
her website: www.lindseyo.com.